ADOBE
PHOTOSHOP
Unmasked

THE ART AND SCIENCE OF SELECTIONS,

LAYERS, AND PATHS

Nigel French

ADOBE
PRESS

Adobe

Adobe Photoshop Unmasked: The Art and Science of Selections, Layers and Paths

Nigel French

Copyright © 2007 by Nigel French

This Adobe Press book is published by Peachpit.

For information on Adobe Press books, contact:
Peachpit
1249 Eighth Street
Berkeley, CA 94710
510/524-2178, 800/283-9444
510/524-2221 (fax)

For the latest on Adobe Press books, go towww.adobepress.com
To report rrors, please send a note to errata@peachpit.com
Peachpit is a division of Pearson Education

Acquisitions Editor: Pamela Pfiffner
Project Editor: Karen Reichstein
Production Editor: Susan Rimerman
Development Editor: Judy Walthers von Alten
Tech Editor: Doug Nelson
Composition: Kelli Kamel
Indexer: Patti Schiendelman
Cover Design: Aren Howell
Cover Production: Andreas Schueller
Cover Photograph: Getty Images

Notice of Rights

Notice of Liability

Trademarks

ISBN 0-321-44120-6

9 8 7 6 5 4 3 2

Printed and bound in the United States of America

Acknowledgments

Many thanks to all the folks at Peachpit Press for making this book possible, especially Pam Pfiffner for commissioning the book in the first place, Karen Reichstein for her graces in smoothing the whole process and for renumbering hundreds of images more times than any person should reasonably have to, Judy Walthers von Alten for her excising any flabbiness in my prose and for teasing out and developing the points I was trying to make, Doug Nelson for his hard-nosed technical edits, Doug Adrianson and Hope Frazier for their excellent copy editing, and Susan Rimerman, production editor. I'd also like to say Cheers to the following people: Joan French, Thespina Coombe, Nadia Proudian, Julian Woodfield and everyone at Media Training; Craig Zeital, the Denley family, Hugh D'Andrade, Tom Erikson, and Monica Pasqual.

TABLE OF CONTENTS

Introduction

Selections, channels, alpha channels, layers, layer masks, shape layers, vector masks, paths, clipping paths, clipping masks. The list goes on. As Photoshop becomes increasingly complex, Photoshop users—even those with years of experience—may feel dizzy with confusion. It's no wonder then that understanding the differences between channels, paths, and layers—and perhaps more importantly, understanding when to favor one approach over another—has become a burning issue for many Photoshop users.

Essential skills for any Photoshop user include making clean, efficient selections, and being able to recall those selections at any time as well as targeting specific areas of an image by tone or color. All of these skills require knowing what to select, and how, whether you're a power or novice Photoshop user. Knowing what to select—and how—is the basis for successfully producing cutouts, photo montages, tonal correction, color correction, or just about anything else you plan to do with an image. Selections and selection techniques—including those that don't use Selection tools—are a useful lens through which to view and understand Photoshop no matter what your level of Photoshop proficiency.

The first, simple premise of this book is that channels, paths, and layers—and their various offspring—are all essentially the same. They all allow you to select and work on specific regions of an image. I use the term *select* in its broadest sense, whether it be in using the Selection tools or Pen tools to isolate part of your image; using any of the myriad layer options to float, move, reveal and conceal, and position parts of a composition independently; or making image adjustments that identify specific tonal or color ranges within an image. With this definition, channels, paths, and layers can all be considered *Selection* tools.

The second premise of this book is that channels, paths, and layers differ significantly. Their features overlap in many areas, but each has its own internal logic and conventions. Channels, paths, and layers allow you to edit your images *selectively* but in different ways and with different results. While a definitive "correct" approach is rare, usually some ways are better, others worse. Understanding how channels, paths, and layers work is crucial to developing an instinct for what the better ways are—that is, the most flexible, efficient, and best-looking approaches to common Photoshop problems. Choosing the appropriate tool can save hours of frustration, and mean the difference between a clean selection and a sloppy selection, a convincing image and an image that looks like it was composited using a rusty hacksaw and wallpaper paste.

Photoshop has evolved radically and beautifully since its launch in 1990. Today's Photoshop offers an unparalleled degree of creative control that is easily learned. But considering all the things you can do with Photoshop, its interface is a marvel of simplicity and intuitiveness. Where confusion exists, it's often because new features have not supplanted old features, but rather peacefully co-exist with them. So, for example, you can still apply image adjustments the "old way," but you're often better off applying them with an adjustment layer. To anyone who has followed the history of Photoshop, this evolution is logical. To those of you who may have skipped a version or two of Photoshop, you probably have some gaps and some areas of confusion.

NOTE: When discussing keyboard shortcuts in the program, I list the Macintosh versions first. In every shortcut used in this book, the Command key translates to the Ctrl key and the Option key translates to the Alt key.

Who Should Read This Book?

To get the most from this book, you should be comfortable working in the Photoshop interface. You should understand basic Photoshop concepts such as using palettes, selecting tools, and applying filters. If you're brand-new to Photoshop, you might do well to pick up a comprehensive book like *Adobe Photoshop CS2 Classroom in a Book* (Adobe Press). If you have some experience working with Photoshop selections, channels, paths and layers, many of the concepts and features explained inside may already be familiar to you. What may not be clear is how they relate to each other, how they are different, and when you should use them. By the time you've read this book, when someone asks, "What's the difference between channels, paths, and layers?" you should have an answer.

How to Use This Book

The chapters are arranged in order of complexity, starting with making basic selections and advancing to making complex channel masks. I'd like it if you started from the beginning and worked your way to the end. But I won't be offended if you just dip in and out to get the information you're after.

web files

The web files icon denotes that a downloadable file is available.

I've included many step-by-step examples throughout the book, and the web files icon denotes that a downloadable file is available. To use these files, download the appropriate chapter folder from the book's companion web site at www.nigelfrench.com/psunmasked. You may also have images of your own that are equally suitable.

Your feedback is important. Feel free to email me with your comments about this book. Tell me what you liked, but also tell me what I got wrong or what I left out.

Nigel French
nigel@nigelfrench.com

ADOBE

PHOTOSHOP
Unmasked

CHAPTER 1

Selections

BECAUSE SO MUCH OF WHAT YOU DO IN PHOTOSHOP begins with a selection, using the Selection tools is a fundamental Photoshop skill. Making selections is about isolating a part, or parts, of your image so that only those parts are affected by what you do next—make a color adjustment, apply a filter, paint, or retouch—to name but a few options.

This chapter examines basic selection concepts and the Selection tools, and their supporting cast of options and menu items used to refine those selections. All of this information is a stepping-stone for more advanced work with alpha channels, layers, and layer masks later in this book. If you're already familiar with Photoshop's Selection tools, you might want to skip this chapter, although I'd recommend at least skimming it because you'll probably pick up a few useful tips.

Some selections are fast and easy, so fast and so easy they may seem like cheating; others take time and patience; others still may be impossible, or, more likely, not worth the effort. While making selections, keep sight of the fact that the unselected parts of the image—those parts you want to protect, or mask, from changes—are just as important as the selected parts.

How you make your selections depends on these main factors:

- **The nature of the selection shape.** Is the subject you want to select a complex or a simple shape? Are its edges soft and delicate or sharp and crisp? Is there good contrast between the subject and its background or is the subject shape murky and ill-defined? Perhaps your subject is all of these things.

- **What you intend to do with the selection.** If you are planning on improving the tonality or color in a region of the image, it may be enough for the selection to be general, sloppy even. If, on the other hand, you plan on cutting out the image and compositing it with another image or images, then you may need to be painstakingly precise.

- **Personal preference.** With many selection options to choose from, people develop their own working style, gravitating towards certain tools and swearing off others. As with just about everything in Photoshop, there are many ways to make selections, and while there is rarely one definitive right way, there are usually better ways, and there are always wrong ways. I'll point out what I feel are the better ways and explain my preferences.

FIGURE 1.1 The basic Selection tools.

Defining Our Terms

Let's begin with a few definitions.

Active selection: Using the Selection tools results in an active selection, which is represented by a flashing outline known as the "marching ants." Looking at an active selection, it's not always easy to tell what parts of the image are selected and what parts are unselected. What's most important is that you are making a boundary between the selected and unselected areas. Should you find you have selected the opposite of what you intended, choose Select > Inverse (Command/Ctrl-Shift-I) to flip your selected and unselected parts of the image.

FIGURE 1.2 A "marching ants" selection of the sky. Note that with marching ants selections it is often difficult to tell what is the selected portion and what is the unselected portion of the image.

Selecting All: The Select > All command (Command/Ctrl-A) selects all the pixels on your active layer. Note that it does not select any pixels beyond the visible portion of your image. This is a pedantic point, so don't worry too much about it, but depending on your Crop tool options it's possible to hide, rather than delete, the cropped portions of your image. In such cases, choosing Select All would not select any pixels that are "hidden" outside the canvas boundaries.

Select
All	⌘A
Deselect	⌘D
Reselect	⇧⌘D
Inverse	⇧⌘I
All Layers	⌥⌘A
Deselect Layers	
Similar Layers	
Color Range...	
Feather...	⌥⌘D
Modify	▶
Grow	
Similar	
Transform Selection	
Load Selection...	
Save Selection...	

FIGURE 1.3 The Select Menu.

Deselecting: If you want to drop or deselect your selection, either select something else or choose Select > Deselect (Command/Ctrl-D).

Reselecting a Selection: If you should accidentally "drop" your selection, so long as it was your most recent selection, you can choose Select > Reselect to get it back.

Inverse Selection: The opposite of the current selection is its inverse. It's often easiest to make a selection by stealth attack, sneaking up on it by selecting the opposite of what you want—usually a solid- or similar-colored background. Then choose Select > Inverse (Command/Ctrl-Shift-I) to get what you're really after. For example, you might select a flat sky or the backdrop to a product shot as a means to selecting the foreground or the product itself.

Hiding and Showing Selection Edges: "Edges" refers to the selection border or marching ants. Because they can be visually distracting, at times you may want to hide them. Choose View > Show > Selection Edges to turn selection edges on and off. Or you can choose View > Extras (Command/Ctrl-H) to toggle on and off all view extras. You can determine exactly what constitutes Extras in the Show Extras Options box available at the bottom of the View > Show menu.

FIGURE 1.4 Inversing a selection. In example **A** I have selected the sky with the Magic Wand, then inversed the selection (example **B**) to select the rocks. The only visible difference is that in example B you can see the marching ants along the edges of the image.

A

B

Feathering: Feathering softens the border of your selection by building a transition boundary between the selection and its surrounding pixels. This can be done for a graphic effect or to create a more natural edge when compositing images. Feathering allows you a certain "fudge factor" by disguising minor inaccuracies in the selection border. When you choose a feather value—the higher the number the softer the border—the softening occurs equally on both sides of the selection border.

A

FIGURES 1.5 Feathering to create a vignette effect. The original, elliptical selection (example **A**). The selection is inversed and the background selected, then feathered 5 pixels (example **B**). Feathered 20 pixels (example **C**). Feathered 40 pixels (example **D**).

B

C

D

TIP: No matter what your level of Photoshop experience, it's easy to forget you have an active selection (most likely a very small portion of your image or a selection whose edges are hidden—View >Show > Selection Edges) and wonder why the image is not responding to your changes. When Photoshop isn't behaving the way you expect, the first thing to check is that you don't have a selection active. If you do, choose Select > Deselect (Command/Ctrl-D).

Anti-aliasing: We take anti-aliasing for granted, but without it all our images would look like they were produced on a Commodore 64 circa 1982, you know—lots of stair-step jaggies. Anti-aliasing prevents jagged selection edges on any kind of curved selections by smoothing the color transition between edge pixels and background pixels. You want Anti-aliasing turned on 99.9 times out of 100.

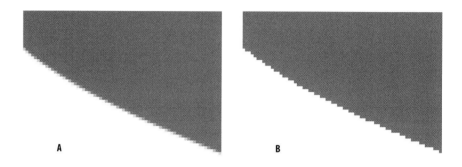

FIGURE 1.6 The same edge anti-aliased (example **A**) and without anti-aliasing (example **B**).

Using the Selection Tools

Each Selection tool has its own strengths and weakness along with a set of options to modify the tool's behavior. The mechanics of using these tools are straightforward; the hard part—or at least the part that takes some experience—is knowing which tool to use and when.

Some basic settings and techniques apply to all the tools.

Presetting Feathering

Before making a selection using a Selection tool, I recommend you set the feather radius to 0 in the options bar. It's always best to start with a clean, unfeathered selection. Feathering, once added, is hard to remove. There is no "unfeather" command. It's all too easy to forget that you have specified a feather amount only to find that you've made selections that are soft when you want them precise.

FIGURE 1.7 In the options bar, it's a good idea to change your feather radius to 0 before making a selection.

Adding to, Subtracting from, and Making Intersecting Selections

When using the Selection tools, mixing and matching is the order of the day. Anything but the most straightforward of selections will require combining Selection tools as well as extending their capabilities with the modifier keys:

- To add to a selection, hold down the Shift key while you use a Selection tool, or click the Add To Selection button in the options bar. A plus sign appears next to the pointer.

- To subtract from a selection, hold Option/Alt while you use a Selection tool or select the Subtract From Selection button in the options bar. A minus sign appears next to the pointer.

- To select an area intersected by other selections, hold down Shift and Option/Alt while you use a Selection tool, or select the Intersect With Selection button in the options bar. An "x" appears next to the pointer.

While adding to and subtracting from are techniques you use every day, intersecting a selection is something done once in a blue moon. And frankly, I can't think of anything it does that using add and subtract can't do more easily. (Although I do use it in Chapter 4 in the "Creating Panoramas" section as a way to intersect the overlapping pixels of two layers.)

A

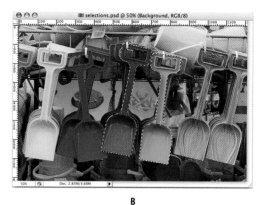

B

C

Add To Selection   Intersect With Selection

New Selection   Subtract From Selection

D

FIGURE 1.8 The red spade is selected (example **A**). Adding to the selection to include the green spade (example **B**). Subtracting from the selection to remove the areas inside the handles (example **C**). The Selection icons from left to right: New Selection, Add to Selection, Subtract from Selection, Intersect with Selection (example **D**).

Moving and Viewing Selections

It's common to want to reposition an active selection without affecting the selection contents. You can do this by clicking and dragging within the selection borders using any of the Selection tools. Alternatively, you can choose a Selection tool and then nudge the selection 1 pixel at a time with the arrow keys; throw in the Shift key and the selection moves 10 pixels at a time.

With marquee selections, i.e. selections made with the rectangular or elliptical marquee tools, you can move the selection while you're still making it by holding down the Spacebar while depressing the mouse button.

To trace a selection edge you need to see it clearly, so view your image at a high enough zoom percentage. And while making a selection (and without releasing the mouse button) you can depress the Spacebar to access the Hand tool and move the image around within the document window.

When a selection includes the edge of the image, it's helpful to see the edge of your canvas and extend your selection outline beyond it. Choose Full Screen Mode with Menu bar (f) and if necessary press Command/Ctrl- to reduce your view size until you see pasteboard around your image. Once outside the image you don't have to be accurate because the selection will snap to the canvas edge when you close the selection.

FIGURE 1.9 Full Screen View mode.

Making Geometric Selections with Marquee Tools

The most basic of the Selection tools, the marquees are used for making geometric selections. Simply drag to select a rectangle or an ellipse. For a perfect square or circle hold Shift while you drag. To draw the selection outwards from the center, hold down the Option/Alt key. Press Shift-M to toggle between the Rectangular and Elliptical Marquee tools.

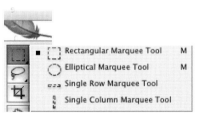

FIGURE 1.10 The Marquee tools.

The less frequently used Single Row and Single Column Marquee tools are used to fix anomalies with screen captures or when making repeating web backgrounds. If you ever need a row of a specific number of pixels you can begin with the Single Row tool, then choose Select > Modify > Expand and expand your selection by the required number of pixels. But frankly it would be easier to use a Fixed Size Marquee (see next page).

Setting Marquee Tool Options

Use the options bar to set the following Marquee tool options:

Feather: For best results, set the Feather amount in the options bar to 0. After you've made your selection, add feathering as needed by choosing Select > Feather (Option/Alt-Command /Ctrl-D).

Anti-alias (Elliptical Marquee only): Unless you have a nostalgic fondness for jagged, stair-stepped selections, always work with this option on.

FIGURE 1.11 The Marquee tool options.

Choose one of the following Style options:

Normal: This option allows unconstrained selections.

Fixed Aspect Ratio: This option constrains your selection to a specified width-height ratio. This is useful if you're preparing several images that you want cropped to the same aspect ratio—something you can't do with the Crop tool without changing the image resolution. Draw your marquee and then choose Image > Crop.

Fixed Size: This option lets you make a selection to a specified size. If the fixed size is bigger than the image dimensions, the selection outline will be outside the canvas. This is distinct from the Crop tool, which lets you crop to specific dimensions while at the same time resampling—that is, adding to or removing pixels from the image.

Selecting by Color with the Magic Wand

The Magic Wand tool is a good choice—the obvious choice—for selecting backgrounds that are relatively flat and contrasting in color with the subject. Once you have the background selected, you can choose Select > Inverse (Command/ Ctrl-Shift-I) to select the subject. Easy-peasy.

The Magic Wand tool selects adjacent pixels based on how similar they are in color (or in shades of gray if you're working with grayscale images or alpha channels). The more similar the pixels, the bigger the selection. The attraction of the Magic Wand is that there's no need to trace a selection outline; just click on the background and all pixels similar in color value are selected.

Don't expect too much from the Magic Wand. When it's good it's really good, but when it's bad—or, more accurately, when it's used badly—the Magic Wand can be a waste of time. If the background varies in color or the edge contrast is slight, the wand is distinctly unmagical. If you don't get the selection you want, it's tempting to increase the Tolerance setting or build the selection by Shift-clicking on the areas that didn't get selected to add them to the selection. Sometimes this will work; sometimes, however, the resulting selection will have ragged edges that result in fringing halos when you modify the selected area. I can't count the number of times I've tried to make a selection with the Magic Wand, hoping (because I'm lazy) that just a few clicks will do the trick, only to find half an hour later that my selection edges look liked they've been cut with a rusty saw. At such times I realize too late that I could have achieved a better result in half the time using the Pen tool (covered later in this chapter), a Quick Mask (Chapter 2, "Channels"), or both.

Setting Magic Wand Options

You can set these Magic Wand tool options in the options bar:

Tolerance determines how much of the image is selected, or, to put it another way, how similar other pixels need to be to the one you clicked. The higher the number, the more pixels are selected. If you don't get everything you want selected when using the Wand, try to set the tolerance higher. But higher tolerance settings (anything above the default of 32), more likely will cause your selection to spill into unwanted areas of your image. Rather than upping the tolerance value, try Shift-clicking with the Magic Wand on the unselected areas to add them to your selection. If you find you're doing this multiple times and you're still not getting what you're after, then the Magic Wand is probably the wrong tool in that situation.

The Magic Wand's tolerance setting is based on the tonal values of the pixels on a scale of 0 (black)–255 (white). With the default tolerance setting of 32, when you click on a pixel the Magic Wand tool selects 32 pixels brighter than that pixel and 32 pixels darker. For example, if you click on a pixel with a tonal value of 50, a range of tonal values between 18 and 82 will be selected. Because most images have more than one color channel (three for RGB, four for CMYK), the tonal value of the pixel is actually the median of all the color channels.

FIGURE 1.12 The Magic Wand tool options.

FIGURE 1.13 Choose the Eyedropper tool (i) to set the Sample Size.

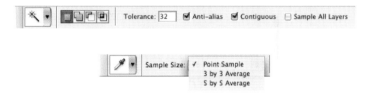

Contiguous selects only adjacent areas with the same color, that is, until dissimilar pixels are encountered. With this option turned off all pixels in the image with similar colors are selected.

A

CRW_4889.CRW @ 50% (RGB/8)

FIGURE 1.14 A Contiguous (example **A**) and a Non-Contiguous (example **B**) selection. The Magic Wand tolerance was set at 32, the default amount.

B

Sample All Layers allows you to select colors from all the visible layers whether they are above or below the active layer. When this is turned off, only colors from the active layer are selected.

How the Magic Wand behaves is also determined by the **Sample Size** specified for the Eyedropper tool. To set the Sample Size, select the Eyedropper tool. With 3x3 or 5x5 Average selected, Photoshop determines the color values by averaging the pixels around the pixel you click. The Point Sample option uses the color value of the actual pixel you click. When working with medium- to high-resolution files, I prefer a 3x3 Average, because with Point Sample it's possible to click a pixel that's atypical of the area you are selecting.

FIGURE 1.15 The sky is relatively flat, making this image a good candidate for a Magic Wand selection. Because there is some color variation in the sky I had to Shift-click with the Wand to add to the initial selection. The tolerance is set at 32.

A

B

FIGURE 1.16 It only takes a few clouds in the sky to throw the Magic Wand tool for a loop. For this selection (example **A**) I had to Shift-click several times with the Wand tool. Even then, on closer inspection (example **B**) it's clear that the selection is far from accurate.

Making Free-Form Selections with Lasso Tools

The Lasso tools are used for making free-form selections of irregular-shaped subjects in images with lots of tonal variations or where the edge of a subject is well defined but the background varies in contrast. In such situations it would be challenging for the Magic Wand tool to make a color-based selection. The Lassos are also great for cleaning up selections. When you want to corral parts of an image that need to be added to or subtracted from an existing selection, the Lasso—as its name suggests—is the tool for the job. To cycle through the tools, press Shift-L.

FIGURE 1.17 The Lasso tools.

Corralling Pixels with the Lasso

With the regular Lasso tool you simply drag around the shape you want to select, making sure you finish where you started.

It's possible to use the Lasso to make detailed and accurate selections if you have a graphic tablet and stylus (more affordable than you might think). But if you're using a mouse or laptop track pad, the Lasso is a blunt instrument, and you should consider a Lasso selection as starting point rather than a total solution. If you're spending hours trying to accurately trace complex selections with the Lasso, then you're working too hard. In fact, the Lasso can be so unwieldy that overusing it is a fast track to repetitive stress injury and frustration. Not to mention shoddy selections. Think of the Lasso as a fast way to get most of the way there. When it comes to accurate tracing along selection edges, you're better off with the Pen tool. But that's just my opinion and there's many a seasoned Photoshop user who would disagree.

You'll make faster, better selections if you know what you intend to do with those selections. Sometimes accurately tracing along an edge isn't necessary. In this example, I wanted to accentuate the flower by darkening its background. Because I knew the selection would be heavily feathered, I could get away with a vague selection shape. I made a rough Lasso selection around the shape and then inversed the selection (Select > Inverse) to select the background. Next, I feathered the selection by 50 pixels (Select > Feather), then darkened the selected area using a Levels Adjustment layer (see Chapter 5, "Adjustment Layers").

FIGURE 1.18A A rough Lasso selection.

FIGURE 1.18B The result of inversing, feathering, and darkening that selection.

The Lasso comes into its own when cleaning up selections that have either spread beyond the intended selection border, or of areas within the intended selection that did not get selected.

FIGURE 1.19 Selecting this leaf should be straight-forward because there is good contrast between subject and background (example **A**). But because the leaf and background vary a lot in tone, a simple Magic Wand selection (example **B**) is only partially successful. In example **C**, the Lasso tool is used to surround the stray pixels. Holding down the Shift key adds them to the existing selection. Example **D** shows the finished selection.

A

B

C

D

If you release the mouse button before tracing all the way around an object with the Lasso tool, the selection is completed with a straight line. Sometimes this can be timesaving if it's unnecessary to draw around the whole object shape. Often, however, this a mistake—and one that may result in a selection line through the center of the object. If that happens, hold Shift and use the Lasso tool again to add to your existing selection and finish drawing around the shape.

Making Straight-Edged Selections with the Polygonal Lasso

Use the Polygonal Lasso tool to draw straight-edged segments of a selection border. You simply position the pointer where you want the first straight segment to end, and click. Continue clicking to set endpoints for subsequent segments. Click back to where you started from to finish the selection; when you position the Polygonal Lasso tool over your starting point a circle appears next to the cursor as an indicator that you're about to finish the selection. Alternatively you can double-click or Command/Ctrl-click from wherever you are to end the selection with a straight segment. The nice thing about the Polygonal Lasso is that you can hold Option/Alt to switch to the regular Lasso at any time, drag the freehand portion of the selection, then release the Option/Alt key and you're back in Polygonal Lasso. (This toggle also works in the Lasso tool, switching you to the Polygonal Lasso tool.)

To draw straight lines at 45° angles, hold down Shift as you move to click the next segment. To erase recently drawn straight segments, press the Delete key. To cancel your selection press Esc.

FIGURE 1.20 The shape of this subject makes it a good candidate for the Polygonal Lasso tool, toggling as necessary to the Lasso by holding Option/Alt to negotiate the non-straight edges.

A

C

B

FIGURE 1.21 In this image (example **A**), I wanted to open up the shadows in the ceiling and along the left wall. In example **B**, because I wanted the brightened areas to blend seamlessly with the rest of the image, I knew I needed to feather the selection a lot, so I didn't worry about drawing around every detail. Just a few clicks were enough to get the selection I needed. In example **C**, this selection became a layer mask for a Curves Adjustment layer, used to bring out the shadow detail in the ceiling. The layer mask was then blurred heavily with the Gaussian Blur filter to blend it in with the image. The same steps were repeated (with slightly less brightening) for the wall. See Chapters 4 and 5 for information on layer masks and adjustment layers.

Snapping to Edges with the Magnetic Lasso

It's pure speculation, but I don't think the Lasso tool was designed to make detailed freehand selections. When the folks at Adobe realized that that's what a lot of people were doing, they decided to help them out with the Magnetic Lasso. This tool snaps to the edges in your image, those areas of your image where there is a discernible difference in the color of the pixels. Sharp edges are easier for the Magnetic Lasso to find; softer, diffused edges are more of a challenge, but you can adjust the tool's options to determine how it "sees" the edge. You just need to gently guide it around the edge—no need to hold down the mouse button. The Magnetic Lasso does the hard work for you, putting down fastening points as you move around the edge. To complete the selection, either click back where you started or double-click to close the endpoints.

Because the Magnetic Lasso tool sometimes has a mind of its own, you'll need to tell it who's boss: At places where the edges lack contrast, clicking to manually add fastening points. You can toggle to the regular Lasso tool by holding Option/Alt and dragging. (Holding Option/Alt and clicking will toggle to the Polygonal Lasso.) Should you go wrong—and you will—press Delete to erase your last fastening point and segment. Each time you press Delete you erase one more fastening point. If things get beyond salvation, press Esc and start from scratch.

FIGURE 1.22 A good candidate for the Magnetic Lasso tool. The edge of the subject is well-defined but the background is of varying contrast. After going around the subject, I made some minor refinements to the selection edge using the regular Lasso tool and using the Magic Wand to subtract pixels where the selection had spilled over the edge.

Setting Magnetic Lasso Options

You can set these options in the options bar:

Feather and Anti-alias As mentioned earlier, I recommend that the feathering for all selection tools be 0 and that anti-aliasing be checked. (These two options are discussed earlier in this chapter).

Width sets how far from the pointer that the Magnetic Lasso tool detects edges. Use a large pixel value width for smooth areas and a small width for more detailed areas. You can vary the width while you're using the tool by pressing] to go bigger, and [to go smaller. If you press Caps Lock before you start drawing the selection, the pointer changes to reflect the width of your edge. Alternatively, you can choose Precise Cursors in your Display & Cursors preferences (Command/Ctrl-K).

Edge Contrast determines the Lasso's sensitivity to edges on a scale from 1% to 100%. The less well-defined the edge, the higher (more sensitive) the setting should be.

Frequency determines how many fastening points are added to the path. For subjects with detailed edges, use higher settings; for less detailed edges, use a lower setting.

Pen Pressure allows you to change the Width if you are using a graphics tablet and stylus.

FIGURE 1.23 The Magnetic Lasso tool options.

Refining Selections

Most selections are made in multiple passes, adding a bit here, deleting a bit there. Let's take a look at some of the options available under the Select menu for refining selections.

When to Feather

Feathering—like so many tasks in Photoshop—can be accomplished in several different ways. What's crucial is not to apply feathering when you make a selection, but rather after the selection is made.

In terms of feathering choices, the Feather menu option is a middleweight, ranking above the Feather option for the Selection tools, but below blurring a mask—the best approach. The Select > Feather command is adequate for many image tasks. Its shortcoming is that the marching ants do not accurately represent how the feather amount will affect the image. Hence you may sometimes see the message "No pixels are more than 50% selected," and no marching ants will appear even though some pixels are partially selected (less than 50%).

A better and more visually interactive way to soften edge transitions is to apply a Gaussian Blur to a Quick Mask, alpha channel, or layer mask. Blurring a mask lets you see how far the feathering spreads, and lets you tweak the feather amount by using the Levels or Curves command on the mask. For a description of this technique, see "Choking a Mask" in Chapter 4, "Layer Masks."

FIGURE 1.24 An unfeathered selection (example **A**). The same selection feathered 40 pixels (example **B**). The unfeathered selection converted to a mask and a Gaussian blur of 40 pixels applied (example **C**).

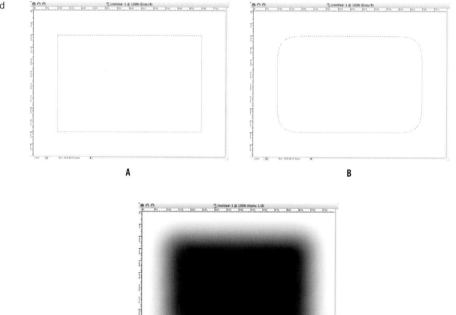

A

B

C

Transforming a Selection

Transform Selection is most useful when working with geometric shapes—for example, when the Rectangular or Elliptical Marquee tool will get you 90% of the way there and you just need to massage the selection shape to get what you're after.

You can choose Select > Transform Selection to scale, rotate, skew, move, or distort an active selection. Transform Selection displays handles around your selection border (like its sibling tool, Free Transform, which transforms the contents of a selection). You then pull the handles to tease your selection into shape. To maintain the proportion of your selection, hold down the Shift key; to transform the selection from the center point, hold down the Option/Alt key, and to distort the selection, hold down the Command/Ctrl key. To accept the transformation, press Enter or click the Commit button in the options bar.

A

B

FIGURE 1.25 A simple Marquee selection is all that's needed to (almost) select this sign (example **A**). Using Transform Selection I held Command/Ctrl and pulled the corner handles to distort the selection shape (example **B**).

Expanding Color Selections

Both the Select > Grow and Similar commands expand a selection to include areas with similar color and by doing such expansions are adjuncts of the Magic Wand tool. Grow includes all adjacent (contiguous) pixels falling within the tolerance range specified in the Magic Wand options, whereas Similar includes all pixels throughout the image (noncontiguous) falling within the tolerance range. Personally, I find it easier to Shift-click with the Magic Wand to add to a selection than to use these options.

FIGURE 1.26 The Modify submenu.

Smoothing a Selection

The Smooth command cleans up stray pixels in a color-based selection. Often when using the Magic Wand tool (or Color Range, discussed in the next chapter) certain pixels that aren't within the tolerance range remain unselected—especially likely if your images are grainy or contain digital noise. Surrounded by swathes of selection these pinholes twinkle like stars in the night sky. A value of 1 to 2 pixels should be sufficient—any higher and you're likely to round off your selection edges too much. Smooth is occasionally useful but it doesn't give you anything you can't get, say, with the Lasso tool. If you're expecting too much from Smooth, then your selection isn't good enough to begin with and you should revisit making a more precise initial selection.

A

B

FIGURE 1.27 This image (example **A**) was scanned from a transparency and is quite grainy. Even after Shift-clicking in the sky several times, numerous unselected pinholes remained. On closer inspection (example **B**), the problem was worse than I'd thought. Choosing Select > Modify > Smooth with a sample radius of 2 pixels (example **C**) does the trick.

C

Contracting or Expanding a Selection

There is almost always a transition between the colors of your selection edge and the background of the image. Sometime these traces of the background color can show up as unwanted color fringe when an image is cut out from its background or composited with another image. One way to eliminate the color fringe is to contract your selection, usually by 1 to 2 pixels. Or, if you are selecting the background, to expand the selection by the same amount. Neither command affects the selection border running along the canvas' edge.

FIGURE 1.28 Here, a selection is made of the flower (example **A**) and then contracted by 2 pixels (example **B**). Examples **C** and **D** show close-ups of the image composited on a background of contrasting color. In example **C**, the selection is not contracted and consequently shows a background color fringe. In example **D**, the selection was first contracted by 2 pixels before being converted to a layer mask. See Chapter 4, "Layer Masks."

Just as with feathering, while the Expand and Contract menu options work just fine, there's arguably a better way to contract ("choke") or expand ("spread") a selection. See a discussion of that technique in Chapter 4, "Layer Masks".

Simulating Anti-aliasing with a Border

You can use Border to smooth the edges of any selections that may have insufficient anti-aliasing. Specifying a border selects a specified number of pixels on either side of the selection edge—making it impossible for you to affect the image outside the lines. Let's say you have an image that's been cut from its background and upon closer inspection you realize that you need to feather the selection edge to help it blend in better with its new background. Choose Select > Modify > Border and specify a width for the border (in the example shown—an 800-pixel-square image—I used a 4-pixel border) and then add a 1-pixel Gaussian Blur (Filter > Blur > Gaussian Blur) to the border selection. To refine this technique it would be preferable to apply the blurring to a layer mask rather than to the image itself. (See Chapter 4, "Layer Masks," for more information on layer masks.)

A

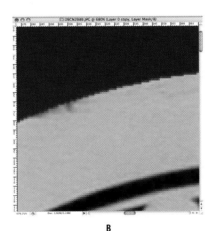

B

C

D

FIGURE 1.29 The original selection (example **A**) shows stair-stepping due to insufficient anti-aliasing (example **B**). A 4-pixel border is added to the selection (example **C**). A 1-pixel Gaussian Blur is applied (example **D**).

Selecting with the Pen Tool

If ever you find yourself stranded on a desert island and are granted one—and only one—Photoshop selection tool (useful on a desert island), my advice is to choose the Pen. It may not always be the fastest or the most convenient, but the Pen tool is the most versatile and—once you've mastered its seemingly strange behavior—the most accurate.

Technically the Pen tool is not really a selection tool. You don't use it to select pixels, but rather to draw paths—mathematically defined lines and curves—around your subjects. Once you have a path, you're just a click away from a selection. The Pen tool is the best choice for making a selection in the following circumstances:

- When the subject is made up wholly or in part of graceful curves or straight edges.

- When the subject is a complex shape set against a low or varying contrast background, ruling out using color-based selection tools.

- When you become exasperated with the Magnetic Lasso tool and its tendency to fly out of control.

The paths we draw in Photoshop (and in Illustrator and InDesign) are made up of Bézier curves, named for their inventor Pierre Étienne Bézier (1910-1999). Bézier was a Renault car company engineer who, in the late 1960s, developed his curves as a way of drawing car body forms on computers. Bézier curves were at the heart of the desktop publishing revolution. They are the basis for vector graphics programs like Adobe Illustrator, and were adopted as the standard curve of Adobe's PostScript page description language. Most outline fonts are stored as Bézier curves.

The Anatomy of a Path

A path consists of path segments (straight line and curve), anchor points, direction points, and control points. The segments make up the path itself. The anchor points determine where the path segment will go. The direction lines, which are manipulated with the direction points, determine the shape of the segment.

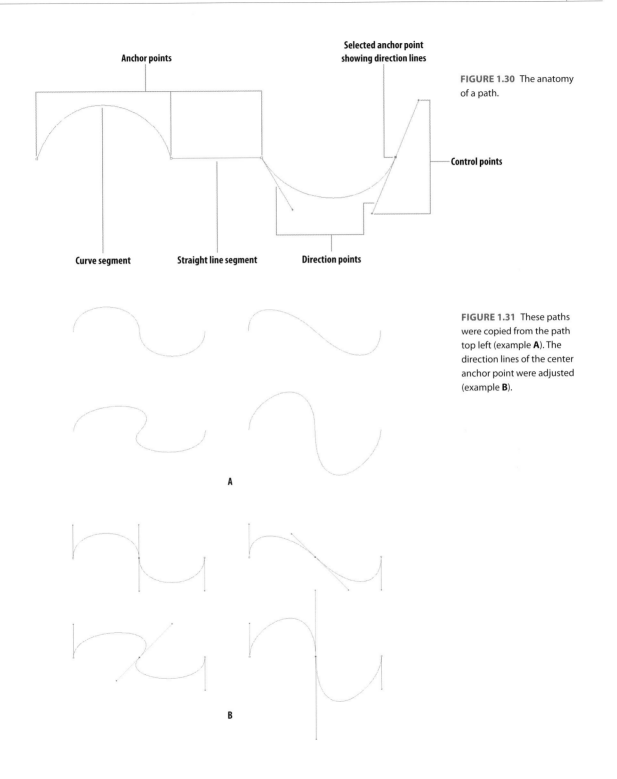

Anchor points

Selected anchor point showing direction lines

FIGURE 1.30 The anatomy of a path.

Control points

Curve segment

Straight line segment

Direction points

FIGURE 1.31 These paths were copied from the path top left (example **A**). The direction lines of the center anchor point were adjusted (example **B**).

A

B

Path segments can be joined by corner points, smooth points, or asymmetrical points.

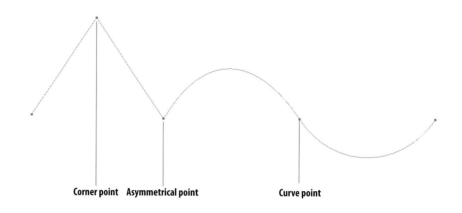

Corner point Asymmetrical point Curve point

Paths can be open or closed. If you turn an open path into a selection, Photoshop will close the two end points with a straight line, so for accurate selections be sure to close the path by clicking again on the first anchor point.

Once you start a path, it appears in the Paths palette as a Work Path, which is temporary and is discarded as soon as you start the next path. If there's even the remotest possibility you'll need the path again, save it by double-clicking Work Path in the Paths palette and giving it a name.

Active paths are displayed as a gray outline, and if a path is active, it will be added to; if no path is active, a new Work Path will be started. This is significant if you're taking several goes to make your path. If you want all your subpaths to be part of the same path, then make sure you activate the path with the Direct Selection tool (so that you can see its anchor points) before you start drawing again.

 A subpath is a series of segments and anchor points created in a discrete Pen tool session. A path around a distinct shape will be made up of a single path; any interior areas will be separate subpaths of the same path.

The Pen Tools

The Pen tool is really the only path tool you ever need, or to be precise the only tool you need choose, because you can access the others by pressing modify keys and specifying Pen tool options—see "Adding and Subtracting Anchor Points" and "Converting Anchor Points" later in this chapter.

The Freeform Pen tool is designed to let you create paths quickly by drawing freehand. If you check the Magnetic Pen option, the Freeform Pen tool behaves like the Magnetic Lasso tool and follows an image edge. If you're new to the Pen tools, the Freeform Pen will likely seem more intuitive, but don't be seduced by its ease of use. It will never give you the Pen tool's degree of control and flexibility. Persevere with the real thing.

FIGURE 1.33 The Pen tools.

To set Pen Tool options, check the Options bar before you start drawing with the Pen. Select the Paths button and verify that the Pen tool is active. The Pen tool's alternative behavior is to create a shape layer—a layer filled with your foreground color and with a vector layer mask (see below) defining the shape of the path you draw. While these can be handy if you need crisp vector shapes, they are no use when drawing paths that you intend to convert to selections. Choose from these options:

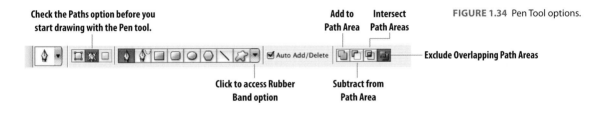

FIGURE 1.34 Pen Tool options.

- Auto Add/Delete allows the Pen tool to automatically switch to the Add Anchor Point tool when positioned over a path segment, or the Delete Anchor Point tool when positioned over an anchor point.

- The Rubber Band option (click the triangle to the right of the shape tools on the Options bar) lets you see where the line is going to be placed before you place it. If you're new to the Pen tool, this may be useful.

FIGURE 1.35 The triangle and semicircle are distinct components of the same path. These four paths have been filled to show the different ways subpaths can interact: Add to path area (example **A**). Subtract from path area (example **B**). Intersect path areas (example **C**). Exclude overlapping path areas (example **D**).

- The four buttons to the right of the Pen tool options determine how subpaths interact with each other.

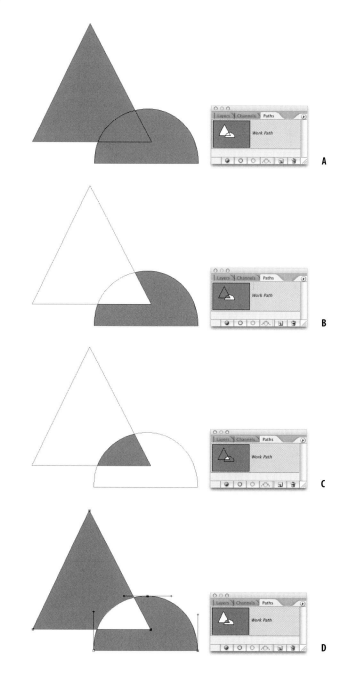

Drawing with the Pen Tool

If you've used the Pen tool before, you may think "drawing" is a misnomer. And you'd be right; you don't so much draw as plot. Click once with the mouse to put down an anchor point, move along the edge you are tracing and click again to put down another, which is joined to the first by a path segment. Simply clicking joins the anchor points with straight-line segments. If, on the other hand, you click and drag you create curve segments. The direction lines that you pull out from the anchor point determine the direction of the curve. As a rule of thumb you need a new anchor point every time the curve changes direction. It feels weird at first, but with practice it makes sense. I promise. And once you get used to it, the Pen tool is really quite therapeutic. Like knitting. You quickly develop a sense of how many anchor points are enough, but when drawing around curve shapes be economical; that way your curves are smooth and graceful.

Here are some useful tips:

- When closing a path, hold down the Option/Alt key as you click again on your first anchor point if you want to prevent your starting anchor point from being converted to a curve point with a second (symmetrical) direction line.

- If drawing a path around a subject that goes to the edge of your canvas, draw your path beyond the canvas edge. If necessary, reduce your view size and expand the document window size to see the pasteboard around your image.

FIGURE 1.36 Because of its graceful curves, I used the Pen tool to draw around this gull. Note how the path continues outside the canvas (example **A**). The path viewed without the image selected with the Direct Selection tool (example **B**). Note how few anchor points are used for the curved segments.

A

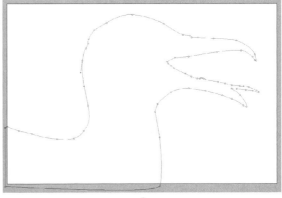

B

■ When adding a new component (distinct section) to a path (for example, to select interior areas of a subject), make sure that the path is active. That way the interior areas will become part of the same path rather than separate paths. If you want the interior areas to be excluded from the resulting selection, make sure you choose the Exclude Overlapping Path Areas button on the Pen options palette—this is the default.

FIGURE 1.37 The image of a doorknocker with pen path drawn around the major shape (example **A**). The pen path viewed by itself (example **B**), and with the interior areas added as components of the same Work Path (example **C**). The Paths palette showing the Work Path thumbnail (example **D**). The path made into a selection (example **E**).

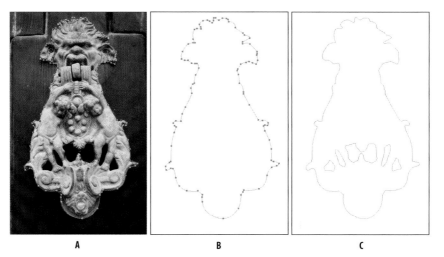

A   B   C

D

E

- For asymmetrical segments—that is, where the direction line affects only one segment—hold down Option/Alt and click the anchor point itself to retract the leading direction line—the one in front of the anchor point. Alternatively, if you are editing an existing segment, click the anchor point with the Direct Selection tool; then hold down the Option/Alt key and drag the control point.

Editing Paths

The key to good pen paths is editing. No one, but no one, gets it right on the first pass. My strategy is to draw around the object quickly and then go back and fix any inaccuracies.

Selecting Paths

There are two selection tools for working with paths:

- **The Path Selection tool** is used for selecting an entire path, if, for example, you want to reposition the path.

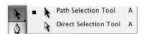

FIGURE 1.38 The Path selection tools.

- **The Direct Selection tool**—the white arrow—is used for editing the shape of a path, either while drawing the path or after the path has been completed. Use the Direct Selection tool to select individual anchor points (you can Shift-click multiple anchors points or draw a marquee over part of the path to edit more than one segment at a time), which you can then drag to reshape the path. You can also drag the control points or the segment itself to change the segment shape. To delete a segment, select it with the Direct Selection tool then press Delete/Backspace. Pressing Delete/Backspace again erases the whole path.

- Access the Direct Selection tool from any Pen tool by holding down the Command/Ctrl key.

- Activate the Path Selection tool when using the Direct Selection tool by holding down the Command/Ctrl key. Alternatively, holding down Option/Alt when in the Direct Selection tool and clicking a path segment will select the whole path.

- Toggle between the Path Selection and Direct Selection tools by pressing Shift-A.

Adding and Subtracting Anchor Points

Editing a path often means adding and subtracting anchor points to the path to gain flexibility in adjusting its shape or to simplify the path. You can use the Add Anchor Point tool and Delete Anchor Point tool, respectively. But if you have the Auto Add/Delete option checked in the Pen Tool options bar, stay in the Pen tool and move your cursor over a line segment or an existing anchor point to add or delete points.

Converting Anchor Points

To convert an anchor point between a corner and smooth point, use the Convert Anchor Point tool, or, if in the Pen tool, hold down the Option/Alt key (if you are in the Direct Selection tool, hold down Command/Ctrl-Option/Alt). To convert a smooth anchor point to a corner anchor point, simply click the point. To change a corner point to smooth, click the point and drag to create direction lines, which are dragged out symmetrically. To retract a direction line, pull it while holding down the Option/Alt key.

Continuing Paths

If you've left an incomplete path and come back to it later, you can add to the path by moving the Pen tool over either endpoint until it turns into the pick up path pointer.

FIGURE 1.39 The pick up path pointer indicates you are about to continue a path.

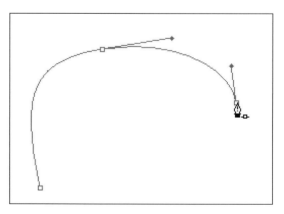

Combining Paths

To combine multiple paths so that you can move them and convert them to a selection as one unit, select the paths with the Path Selection tool, and from the Options Bar, click the Combine button. Now when you move one path, all the combined paths move right along with it.

Transforming Paths

Just as with raster graphics, you can transform paths using the individual transform options under the Edit menu or by using the one-stop-shop for transformations: Free Transform (Command/Ctrl-T).

Using the Paths Palette

The Paths palette is the control center for working with paths. The illustration shows its key features.

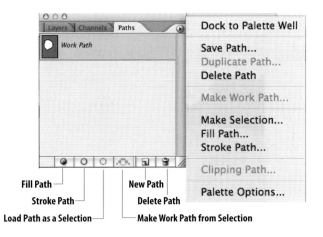

FIGURE 1.40 The Paths palette. Even if you plan to convert your path to a selection, it's worth saving a path as insurance—and paths add little to your file size.

Make Selection

The most useful item on the Paths palette menu is Make Selection. Once you've defined an accurate path you can convert it to a selection. And why the extra step? Because paths are not actually selections but vector outlines and consequently don't allow feathering and anti-aliasing of their edges. To make a selection using the last settings specified in the Make Selection dialog box, Command/Ctrl-click the Make Selection icon at the bottom of the Paths palette. Hold down a modifier key if you want the new selection to be added to (Shift), subtracted from (Option/Alt) or to intersect (Shift-Option/Alt) an existing active selection.

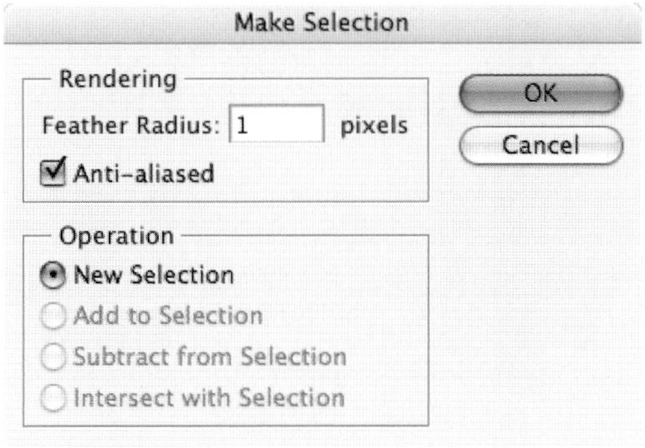

FIGURE 1.41 Using Make Selection you can specify a feather radius and determine how the selection interacts with an existing active selection.

As well as being able to turn a path into a selection, you can also go in the other direction. Any selection can be turned into a Work Path using the Make Work Path icon at the bottom of the Paths palette. A lower tolerance number gives a more accurate but more complicated path. If a selection has rather jagged edges, using a higher tolerance can smooth the path. However, you'll always get a better result drawing the path yourself rather than converting a selection to a path.

Stroking a Path

Choose Stroke Path from the Paths palette menu to use the Painting or Retouching tool to stroke an active path. Click the Stroke Path icon at the bottom of the Paths palette and the active tool in the Toolbox (if it's capable of stroking a path) is used with its current settings. If the active tool can't be used, the tool last selected to stroke a path is used.

But why do this? While it isn't something I do often, it does have some effective uses. For example, you can stroke a path with the Clone tool or Healing Brush to repair or retouch a continuous line of blemish like a power line. Let's look at an example.

A   B

FIGURE 1.42 The original image (example **A**) and the finished image (example **B**) with the neon "turned on" by stroking a pen path.

1. Open the source image, Neon. In this example I used Stroke Path to "light up" the neon in this sign (the real neon was broken).

2. Draw the path. Once you've finished, double-click the Work Path to save the path.

web files

FIGURE 1.43 The path drawn around the neon (all subpaths are shown selected).

3. From the Layers palette menu, choose New Layer to add a new layer to the image. This way the added paint will be independent of the background layer. Name the layer "Stroke."

NOTE: An active path may show just the path outline. If you select it with the Path Selection tool, all anchor points on the path are solid; if you select it with the Direct Selection tool, the anchor points are hollow.

4. Select a bright red color from the Swatches palette. Choose your Brush tool (b) and a 10-pixel brush with 0% hardness.

5. Make sure that the path is active and click the Stroke Path icon on the Paths palette to stroke the path.

6. To complete the effect, reduce the opacity of the Stroke layer and apply a Gaussian Blur filter.

Stroking a path can also help you get the best from the Extract tool. This technique is discussed in Chapter 6, "Channel Masks."

Clicking the Fill Path with the foreground color icon at the bottom of the Paths palette does exactly that—equivalent to making a selection and filling it with the foreground color. If you want filled vector shapes, use a shape layer instead, which assigns your shape to its own layer for more editing flexibility.

Making a Clipping Path

Clipping paths can be used to define transparent areas in images that you are exporting to page layout applications. When you import the image into your page layout, the area outside the clipping path is invisible. However, now that the current versions of InDesign and QuarkXPress recognize "real" transparency—as defined by an alpha channel or a layer mask—old school clipping paths are arguably obsolete. Because alpha channel and layer masks are 8-bit, or, to put it another way, because they support 256 shades of gray, you can feather their edges as well as vary their opacity. Clipping paths, on the other hand, are hard-edged and historically have been responsible for too many "blunt scissor" masks. So, do you ever need a clipping path? Well, perhaps. Clipping paths have an advantage in two respects:

- Sharp, crisp edges are preferable when masking some objects.
- Clipping path file sizes are smaller than layer mask files.

Once a path is saved it can be defined as a clipping path by choosing Clipping Path from the Paths palette menu. Its' name will be outlined. When the file is saved and imported into a page layout program the area outside the clipping path is masked. However, rather than use the Clipping Path option from the Paths palette menu, opt instead for a Vector mask, whose effects you can evaluate and edit within Photoshop. See "Vector Masking Sharp Edges" in Chapter 4.

In Summary

Here's the thing with the Selection tools: they're fast and convenient, but as I mentioned earlier, they're a bit blunt. Sometimes, depending on your intent, an accurate selection may not be necessary and a general selection will suffice. Sometimes what you need to select will be a rectangular or elliptical shape or a shape conveniently made up of nice straight-sided segments. Other times you will need to make selections of subjects that twist and turn, are sometimes crisp and sometimes vague, and that are shot against backgrounds that offer little or no contrast. When working with such images, the selections you make with the Selection tools are a start, but that's all they are. The Lassos, Marquees, and the Magic Wand will get you 90% of the way there, but for that remaining 10% (which always takes way more than 10% of the time), you'll need to use Quick Masks, which we'll cover in the next chapter.

CHAPTER 2

Channels

BEFORE THERE WERE LAYERS, before layer masks and adjustment layers, before clipping masks, Smart Objects, and all the other selection-related features that Photoshop offers today, there were channels. And as impressive as those features are, they can never supplant channels in terms of their fundamental importance. Channels underpin every Photoshop image you work with, and working in Photoshop you're working with channels whether you know it or not.

Every image is made up of channels—or a single channel if it's a grayscale, bitmap, or indexed color image—and utilizing those channels will vastly expand your range of image-editing possibilities and massively speed up your workflow. Channels come in three flavors: color channels, which store the color information in our images; alpha channels, which are saved selections; and spot color channels, which expand our range of printing options.

Color channels store information about the color of each pixel in your image. The most common way to describe a pixel's color is in RGB—red, green, blue—although as we'll see there are other ways. Much as you might mix paints on a palette to create a range of colors, Photoshop mixes red, green, and blue in different proportions to represent the colors in an image. Every pixel in an RGB image has three numbers that describe its red, green, and blue components. Collectively, the red values for all the pixels in an image make up the Red channel. The same is true of the green and blue values and their channels.

FIGURE 2.1 The composite channel (example **A**) is made up of three channels in an RGB image (examples **B** and **C**) and four in a CMYK image (example **D**). The number of color channels depends on the color mode of an image.

How many color channels an image starts out with is determined by its color mode—three for RGB, four for CMYK. For example, when you open an RGB image, it's made up of three channels: Red, Green, and—you guessed it—Blue, superimposed on each other. A fourth, composite channel (RGB) allows you to view all three color channels together. You can also view the channels individually or in combination. Let's take a look at this deconstructed image.

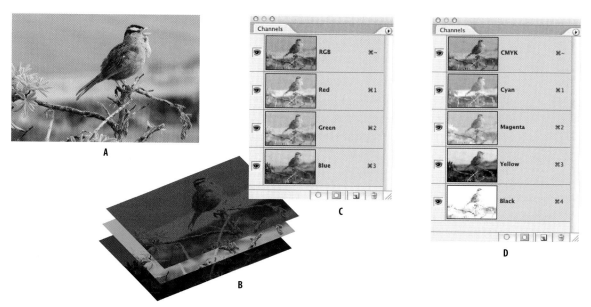

If you're familiar with how offset printing works, you can think of channels as printing plates, with a separate plate applying each channel of color. In addition to color channels Photoshop has two other types of channels: the absolutely essential alpha channels, for saving selections, and the occasionally useful spot color channels, for expanding the range of printing options.

An understanding of channels is the foundation for working with all selection tools in Photoshop. Here's what channels can do for you:

- You can save selections as alpha channels. Don't be put off by the name, alpha channels are nothing more than potential selections, which you can load on an as-needed basis. Like stencils, alpha channels are black-and-white representations of what is selected in the image (white) and what is unselected or masked (black).

- You can use channels to create more accurate selections than is possible with Selection tools. By converting a selection to a Quick Mask (see "Using Quick Masks to Paint Selections" later in this chapter), you can refine it with your painting tools and then convert it to a (permanent) alpha channel.

- You can use channels for more than just storing selections. In this chapter, we'll see how you can optimize Web images by compressing specific parts of an image and so reduce their download time, as well as how to mix channels to create high-quality grayscale images.

- You can create a duotone to allow you to print with a limited number of inks as well as to extend the tonal range of a printed image.

- You can create spot color channels to specify additional plates for printing with spot color inks. For example, you can create specific print effects using a channel to apply a spot (custom color) ink or varnish—such as for a logo or to make a particular color "pop" on the page—that will print to a separate plate.

- You can use channels as the starting point for making complex selections. Often the selection you want to make is right there, in the channel, waiting to be teased out. The best approach to selecting images with fine-edge detail, like hair, fur, tree branches, and so forth, is to make a duplicate of one of your existing color channels and then refine this channel to make your mask. This technique is the subject of Chapter 6, "Channel Masks."

NOTE: With the evolution of layers, layer masks, and adjustment layers (discussed in Chapters 3, 4, and 5 respectively) some of the things that you could previously only achieve with channels—such as gradient masks or combining channel blend modes with Calculations—are now more easily, and more safely, achieved with layers. For example, layer masks are channels that are applied to specific layers and can be used to make nondestructive, that is, reversible changes. An understanding of channels is the foundation for working with all masking tools in Photoshop.

About Channels

When you open an image, the composite channel is selected, and that's where you do most of your editing to an image. When viewed individually, channels—even color channels—are displayed as grayscale images. You have the preference of viewing your color channels in color, but this is not as useful as it may sound (see the following section, "Using the Channels Palette").

Those of you into Photoshop numerology will be interested to know that you can have as many as 56 channels (57 including the composite channel). Common sense, however, will ensure that you use far fewer. Adding channels to your document will increase its file size, although not significantly; the more important issue is that too many channels will likely cause confusion. By default, bitmap, grayscale, duotone, and indexed color images have one channel; RGB and lab images have three; and CMYK images have four. Alpha channels are saved with the document.

In addition to the built-in color channels you can, throughout the course of editing an image, add additional channels, called alpha channels. Despite the highfalutin name, these are nothing more than saved selections. Because they are saved selections, alpha channels can be recalled, viewed, and edited at any time. Alpha channels do not print.

Once you've gone to the trouble of making a selection, it's a good idea to save it as an alpha channel (Select > Save Selection...), so that you don't need to make the selection all over again the next time you want to edit that same portion of your image. Alpha channels are also referred to as masks. But whether you're calling them alpha channels, saved selections, or masks, they are the same thing: a grayscale representation where the white pixels represent the editable (selected) areas, the black pixels the protected (unselected, or masked) areas, and the gray pixels, if there are any, the partially selected areas.

NOTE: Not all color modes use multiple channels—bitmap, grayscale, and indexed color modes use a single channel.

NOTE: This "white: editable; black: masked" relationship can be reversed in your Channel Options. Don't worry about it: what's important is that the channel defines a separation between the areas of your image that you want to affect and those that you want to protect. If it turns out that your alpha channel actually defines the opposite of what you need, then either Invert the channel (Image > Adjustments > Invert or Command/Ctrl-I) or, if the selection is active, make an inverse of the selection by choosing Select > Inverse or Command/Ctrl-Shift-I.

A third, less frequently used type of channel is a spot color channel, used to specify an additional plate for printing with spot color inks. When it comes to printing on a printing press, Photoshop is essentially a four-color program; that is, when preparing images for printing on a printing press the colors in your image are made up of varying percentages of cyan, magenta, yellow, and black. If you need to print with specific spot colors—either because your job will be printed on a low budget, for example, a two-color print job that uses black plus a second specified spot color, or because you need to accurately match a color from a corporate logo or brand imagery—then you need a spot color channel.

NOTE: Not all file formats support alpha channels. JPEG, for example, does not. To save your alpha channels with your image, save your file in Photoshop, PDF, PICT, Pixar, or TIFF formats. To save spot color channels, use Photoshop or DCS 2.0.

FIGURE 2.2 A simple spot color image (example **A**) designed to print in only two colors (example **B**).

A

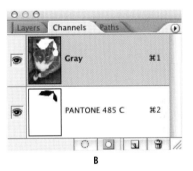

B

Using the Channels Palette

The Channels palette is where you can add, delete, edit, and view channels. The palette lists all channels in the image, with the composite channel at the top.

FIGURE 2.3 The Channels palette showing the composite channel (top), the three color channels (Red, Green, Blue), and the palette menu.

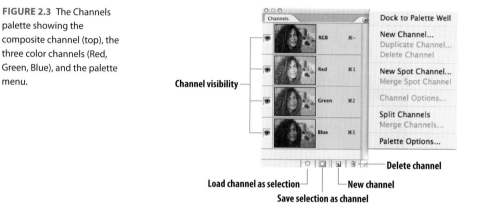

Individual channels are shown in grayscale. If you'd prefer to see your color channels in their respective colors (red, green, and blue or cyan, magenta, yellow, and black) choose Command/Ctrl-K to bring up Photoshop Preferences. Then from the pop-up menu at the top left, choose Display & Cursors to view those preferences. While this might be useful to help conceptualize how the color channels add up to the sum of their parts, it's of little practical use because it is in grayscale that we can most clearly evaluate the tonal values of the color components our color channels. Once the novelty of seeing your individual channels in color has worn off, I'd recommend going back and unchecking this preference.

FIGURE 2.4 You can opt to view your channels and channel thumbnails in color rather than grayscale.

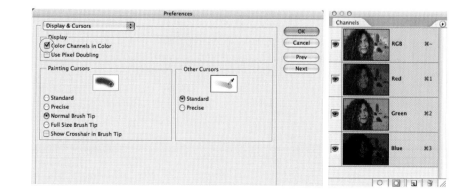

Viewing and Editing Channels

In the Channels palette, you can select one or more channels for editing. The names of all selected, or active, channels are highlighted. Any changes you make apply to the active channels; channels that are not active are not affected. This ability to edit specific channels is significant because it's another way of applying changes selectively. For example, when applying a filter to an image, you might not want all channels affected. In an RGB image the Blue channel typically has more noise or grain than the Red or the Green channels. Typically, the Red channel has the most contrast, and the Green the most detail. Applying an Unsharp Mask filter to the Red and the Green channels, but not to the Blue, is a way of sharpening only the details that you want sharp and avoiding accentuating the noise or grain. See the section, "Sharpening Images by Isolating Channels."

To show or hide a channel, click in the eye column in the Channels palette next to the channel. To select a channel, click its thumbnail. Hold down the Shift key to select multiple channels. To show or hide multiple channels, drag through the eye column in the Channels palette. Click the composite channel to display all the color channels. You can also use key shortcuts to select channels: Command/Ctrl-1, 2, 3, to select Red, Green, Blue, respectively (Command/Ctrl-1, 2, 3, 4 if you are in CMYK mode). Command/Ctrl 4 (or 5 in CMYK) will select your first alpha channel and so on. To select the composite channel press Command/Ctrl-~ (tilde).

Here's an interesting thing: Individual channels appear in grayscale, but if you are viewing a combination of channels, they appear in color, whether or not you are viewing your channels in color.

If you display an alpha channel at the same time as color channels, the alpha channel appears as a transparent color overlay, like a sheet of acetate. The default percentage and color of this overlay is 50 percent red, which works well much of the time, but is about as useful as a chocolate teapot if you're working on an image that has lots of red in it. In such cases you can change the overlay color by double-clicking the alpha channel thumbnail in the Channels palette to display the Channel Options dialog box and change the color.

FIGURE 2.5 An active selection.

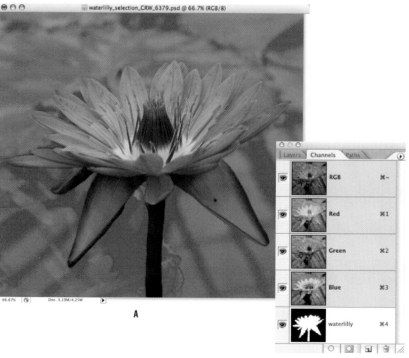

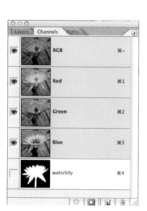

FIGURE 2.6 That selection saved as an alpha channel, viewed in the Channels palette.

FIGURE 2.7 The alpha channel viewed as a mask, indicated by a transparent red overlay on top of the image (example **A**). Note the visibility eyeballs in the Channels palette (example **B**).

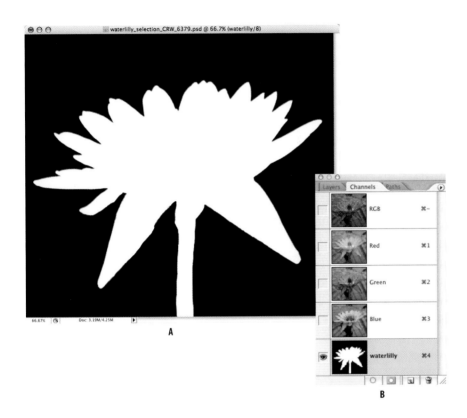

A

B

FIGURE 2.8 The alpha channel viewed by itself (example **A**). Note the single visibility eyeball in the Channels palette (example **B**).

FIGURE 2.9 Double-click the channel thumbnail to bring up the Channel Options.

Because alpha channels are grayscale images, you can edit them as any other image by using painting tools, selection tools, and filters. You paint on an alpha channel in black or white or shades of gray (if a color swatch is selected in the Toolbox, the color is converted to a grayscale value). Press the x key to toggle your foreground and background colors. By default, if you paint in white you add to the selected area; if you paint in black you add to the unselected or masked area—although you can invert this relationship, as shown in the Color Indicates portion of the Channel Options dialog box in Figure 2.9. Painting with white or black at an opacity of less than 100%, that is, painting in gray, partially selects the area. Note that when you load an alpha channel as a selection, the marching ants can only represent pixels that are more than 50% selected. So in terms of accurately representing what's selected and what's not, channels beats the ants.

NOTE: Deleting a color channel converts the image to Multichannel mode. Because Multichannel mode does not support layers, all visible layers are flattened and hidden layers are discarded.

Saving Selections as Channels

As I've already mentioned, once you've made a selection, whether it's a simple selection or complex one, you don't want to have to make it all over again the next time you work on that portion of the image. So save it—and once it's saved, you can recall it instantly. To save an active selection, choose Select > Save Selection, choose the appropriate options, and click OK.

FIGURE 2.10 The Select menu (example **A**) and Save Selection options (example **B**).

A

FIGURE 2.11 Saving selections using the Channels palette.

Save selection as channel

Alternatively, you can save time and bypass the Select menu altogether: with your selection active, just click on the Save Selection as Channel icon at the bottom of the Channels palette. The channels will be called Alpha 1, Alpha 2, and so on. If you want to rename a channel, just double-click its name in the Channels palette to rename it in place.

Loading a Saved Selection

To recall a saved selection, choose Select > Load Selection. (Typically you load a selection from one document into the same document, but you can also load a selection from any open document by choosing its name from the Document pull-down menu.) If you already have another selection active, you can specify whether you want the selection that you are loading to be added to, subtracted from, or intersected with that selection. Alternatively, just drag the channel thumbnail onto the Load Channel as Selection icon at the bottom of the Channels palette. Hold down the appropriate modifier keys if you want the channel you are loading to combine with your current active selection: Shift to add,

Option/Alt to subtract, Option/Alt-Shift to intersect. I prefer to load my selections in this way, although I do not have the option, as I would with the Load Selection dialog, of inverting the selection at the same time. You can also load selections by Command/Ctrl-clicking the channel thumbnail.

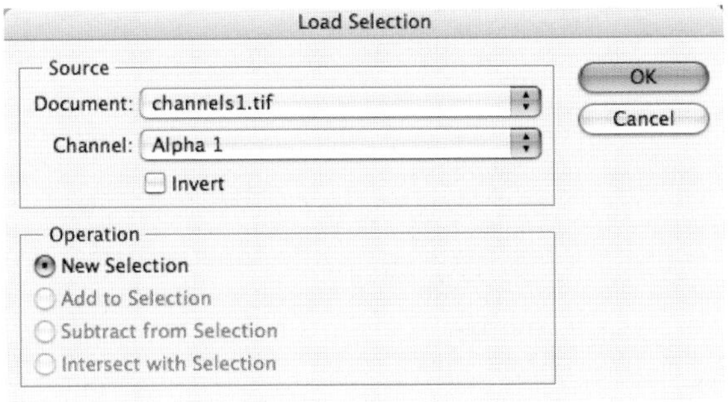

FIGURE 2.12 The Load Selection dialog. If you have more than one alpha channel, you can choose which one to load using the Channel pull-down menu. The Operation buttons give you the option of combining or subtracting the alpha channel with an active selection. Check Invert to inverse the selection (same as choosing Inverse from the Select menu).

Once the selection is active, you can edit the size and shape of the selection with any of your selection tools. Saving this new selection again will not overwrite your current channel, because each time you save a selection as a channel, a new alpha channel is created and added to the Channels palette. If you want to update your existing channel rather than create a new channel, you can choose Select > Save Selection > Add to Channel and select the original channel from the pull-down menu. Personally I find it quicker to create a new channel and then delete any old channels I no longer need by dragging their thumbnails to the Trash icon at the bottom of the Channels palette.

Updating a Saved Selection

You can also replace, add to, subtract from, and intersect with any existing saved selection. For example, if you have already saved a selection and you wish to update it, load the existing selection as above, make your changes to the selection, then choose Select > Save Selection. From the Channel pull down menu, choose your saved selection and choose the appropriate operation.

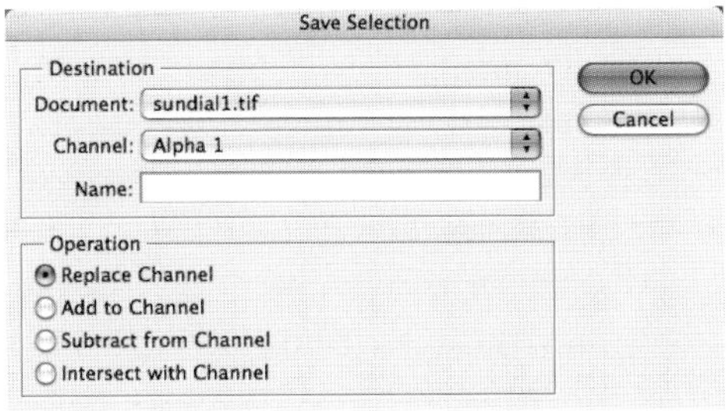

FIGURE 2.13 Replace an existing alpha channel with your updated selection.

Using Quick Mask to Paint Selections

Now we've got the formalities out of the way, let's see how we make channels work for us. First, let's look at Quick Mask, which is somewhere between a selection and an alpha channel. Like a selection, it goes away when not in use; like in an alpha channel, you can see a transparent color overlay on top of your image representing the masked areas of the image. A Quick Mask channel will show up in the Channels palette—but only when it's active. And you can edit the shape of that mask with your painting tools or filters. This is the punch line: when making complicated selections, you can be more accurate using painting tools on a Quick Mask rather than using your basic selection tools.

The thing about Quick Mask is that it's, well, quick. And temporary. You turn a selection into a Quick Mask so that you can refine it as a color overlay mask, and then turn it back into a selection when you're done. From there, you can save the refined selection as an alpha channel (or a layer mask). Strictly speaking, Quick Masks don't give us anything we don't already have with alpha channels—they're just more convenient.

Some people love Quick Masks and use them every day. I have to confess that I don't use them often. Quick Masks are stepping-stones to creating something else, most likely an alpha channel or a layer mask. I prefer to cut out the middle step and go directly to one of these options—both of which result in a saved mask—because you never know when you might need to go back and refine that mask. A word of caution about Quick Masks: as handy as painting on a mask can be, I bet that every time you find yourself spending hours on a complex mask you're thinking, "There has to be a better way." Well, usually there is. If you want total control over the shape of your edges, there's no substitute for the Pen tool, covered in Chapter 1, "Selections." And for images with fine-edge detail, like hair, fur, tree branches, and so forth, you're better off making a channel mask, which is covered in Chapter 6, "Channel Masks."

As I mentioned in the previous chapter, your basic Selection tools are a starting point; Quick Masks are for refining selections. Once you have made your starting selection, click the Quick Mask button in the Toolbox to switch to Quick Mask mode. In Quick Mask mode, you can partially select areas of your image by painting with gray, as well as feather parts of your selection by varying the softness of your brush as you paint. If you turn off all other channels in the Channels palette, you can view your Quick Mask as grayscale information and continue to refine it there by painting in black or white.

Let's take a look at a practical example.

1. Open the Car image.

web files

A

B

FIGURE 2.14 The original image (example **A**) and the masked image cut out using a Quick Mask (example **B**).

2. Begin by drawing a Pen path around the car or click on Path 1 in the Paths palette to use the Pen path that is saved with the image. From the Paths palette menu, choose Make Selection to convert the Pen path to an active selection. I chose a feather radius of 0.5 pixel.

   I chose the Pen because of the curves and straight lines that make up most of the car shape. Pen paths are discussed in Chapter 1.

3. Click the Quick Mask icon at the bottom of the Tools palette (or press Q). My Quick Mask color was green from the last time I used it, and that works fine; yours will probably be red. If you want to change the color of the mask, double-click the Quick Mask button to bring up the Quick Mask Options dialog. Note that the swatches in the Toolbox automatically become black and white when you switch to Quick Mask mode.

FIGURE 2.15 Click the Quick Mask icon to enter Quick Mask mode (example **A**). Double-click the Quick Mask icon to bring up the Quick Mask Options (example **B**).

You might like to Option/Alt click the Quick Mask icon to toggle between the overlay color showing the masked areas and the selected areas. Remember, what's most important is that you're making a distinction between the subject and its background.

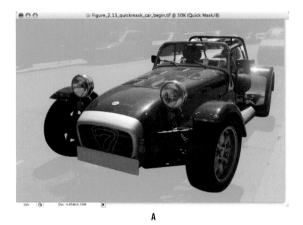
A

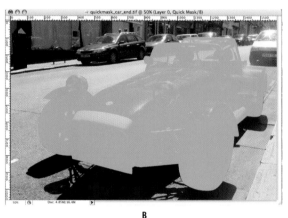
B

FIGURE 2.16 The image in Quick Mask mode with the color showing masked areas (example **A**) and selected areas (example **B**). I found it most useful to move back and forth between these two views by Option/Alt-clicking the Quick Mask icon.

4. Choose the Paintbrush and refine the edges of the mask. Zoom in to a comfortable view size so that you can clearly see the edge detail. If you have the color set to indicate the selection, paint with black or, if the color indicates the masked areas, paint with white to select more of the image (the color overlay is removed from areas painted with white). Painting with gray or another color creates a semitransparent area, useful for feathering or anti-aliased effects. (Semitransparent areas may not appear selected when you exit Quick Mask mode, but they are.)

5. Finally, when you are satisfied with your Quick Mask, switch back to Standard mode. Your mask becomes a selection, and you can save it as an alpha channel or edit it the way you want.

In my case, I converted the selection to a layer mask (see Chapter 4, "Layer Masks") to hide the foreground area. To do this, press Option/Alt and double-click the layer thumbnail of the Background layer and then click the Layer mask icon at the bottom of the Layers palette. As an optional finishing step I added a simple drop shadow by choosing Drop Shadow from the Layer Styles pull-down menu at the bottom of the Layers palette. Layer styles are discussed in Chapter 3, "Layers."

Masking Tips

Here are some tips that are equally applicable whatever kind of mask you are working on: a Quick Mask, alpha channel, or a layer mask (see Chapter 4 for more information on layer masks).

- Ask yourself why. Be sure to ask yourself what you are making that mask for. Depending on your intent, it may not even be necessary to make a mask. Can you select the areas of the image you want by color, by tone, using a layer blend mode? (see Chapter 3 for more on layer blend modes.) It's all too easy to get carried away with making complex masks just because you can. Don't lose sight of your objective.

- In Quick Mask mode, you can toggle back and forth between the overlay, indicating the masked areas and the selected areas by Option/Alt-clicking the Quick Mask icon. In Quick Mask mode, sometimes it may be helpful to press Q to toggle between Standard mode and Quick Mask to see what your selection looks like as marching ants compared with a Quick Mask overlay. Note that the marching ants can't display pixels that are less than 50% selected. If your mask is feathered, the marching ants indicate the transition between pixels that are less than 50% selected and those that are more than 50 percent selected change your perspective.

FIGURE 2.17 Different ways of seeing the same information: marching ants, Quick Mask, and alpha channel.

- Change your brush size, opacity, and hardness as necessary as you paint in the mask. The methods for painting a mask are the same whether you're working on a Quick Mask, an alpha channel, or a layer mask.

■ You can continue to use your basic selection tools as well as your filters while you are editing in Quick Mask mode or touching up an alpha channel or layer mask. For example, rather than paint in large interior areas of your subject with your painting tools, it may be more efficient to make a selection with one of your Lasso tools. With these, you can stay away from any difficult edges, and then fill this selection with black or white, depending on whether you are adding to the masked areas or to the selected areas.

■ If you've tried accurately painting the edge of a mask in Quick Mask mode, you might be thinking that it's as hard to be accurate with a paintbrush as it is with a Lasso. And you'd be right. But painting on a mask comes into its own when you get clever about the kind of brush you use. If you are working on a high-contrast edge—perhaps an edge that has lots of intricate detail making it hard to select with your basic selection tools—painting along the edge in the Overlay blend mode can get great results. Painting in white pixels lighten only those pixels that are less than 50% gray. Painting in black darkens only those pixels that are more than 50% gray.

FIGURE 2.18 Painting along the edge of the mask (example **A**) in Overlay blend mode (example **B**) to increase contrast.

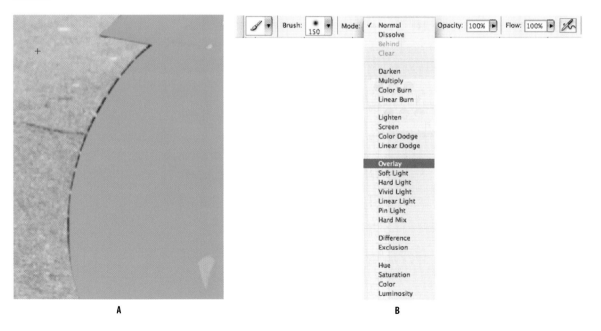

A   B

Fine-Tuning Color Selections

In the previous chapter we saw how we can use the Magic Wand tool for making color-based selections. Sometimes there's a better way.

Using Color Range to Make Complex Color-based Selections

Color Range is actually a Selection tool, but I've included it in the Channels chapter because you're better equipped to use Color Range effectively once you understand how channels work. The Color Range feature uses a channels-like interface to show you which pixels are selected and which pixels are protected. It allows you to create a more sophisticated mask than you could achieve with the Magic Wand tool.

Like the Magic Wand tool, Color Range makes selections based on the similarity of color values; its selections are noncontiguous. But the Color Range preview window gives a better indication of which pixels will be selected than the simple marching ants outline that results from a Magic Wand selection. And whereas the Magic Wand tool either selects or does not select a pixel, Color Range allows you to partially select pixels—just like painting on a mask with gray.

Color Range is the Swiss Army knife of selection tools. In addition to making selections by sampling colors with the eyedroppers, you can also make selections based on specific colors or tonal ranges or out-of-gamut colors. This is especially useful if you are working with an image where you want to change the hue of a particular color, affect only the shadows or only the highlights, or desaturate out-of-gamut colors to bring them back into the range of printable colors.

Choose Select > Color Range and click with the eyedropper on the pixels you want to select. To extend the range of colors, select the plus eyedropper (or hold down Shift), and click in the preview area or image. To remove colors, select the minus eyedropper (or hold Option/Alt), and click in the preview area or image. When the Selection button is checked, your selection is previewed in the Color Range dialog box like a grayscale alpha channel. While I've never found any reason to change this, you can, if you wish, see your selection preview in the image window and choose from the Selection Preview drop down menu to view the selection as Grayscale, against a black or white matte, or as a Quick Mask. The Fuzziness slider is roughly equivalent to the Magic Wand's Tolerance setting but allows pixels to be partially selected. Move the slider to the right to increase the size of the selection.

Note that you might get better results if you first make a rough selection before choosing Color Range.

FIGURE 2.19 The Color Range tool. Selected areas of the image appear in white, masked areas in black, partially selected areas in gray.

FIGURE 2.20 Click with the eyedropper on the image to sample the pixels you want to select. Use the plus eyedropper to extend the selection, the minus eyedropper to remove pixels from the selection. Move the Fuzziness slider to the right to expand the selection or to the left to shrink the selection.

FIGURE 2.21 The resulting selection as represented by marching ants (example **A**), and after smoothing by 2 pixels and cleanup with the Lasso tool (example **B**).

A

B

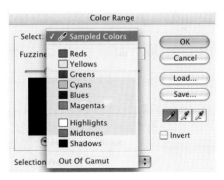

FIGURE 2.22 You can use Color Range to select more than just sampled colors.

Color Range Versus the Magic Wand

This image of Delicate Arch was shot with low light and scanned from a transparency on a midrange slide scanner. Consequently, there's a lot of grain, especially in the Blue channel, which, not surprisingly, is showing up most in the sky. I want to mask the sky so that I can make a tonal correction on the foreground. I also want to sharpen just the foreground so that I don't accentuate any of the graininess in the sky.

FIGURE 2.23 The original image (example **A**) and the image edited using a mask to selective sharpen and improve the tonal range (example **B**).

A

B

1. Open the Arches image.

FIGURE 2.24 Using the Magic Wand for this kind of selection yields a very raggedy selection.

2. Choose Select > Color Range. To see a selection take shape in the Color Range dialog box, I prefer the Color Range previews set to Selection and Selection Preview set to None. Click with the eyedropper on an area of sky in the image; these areas will become white in the preview to indicate they are selected. Shift-click on any areas of sky that were not included in the initial selection. Dragging the Fuzziness slider up and down will expand or shrink the selection—I used a Fuzziness of about 70. When you have a good—not perfect—separation between sky and foreground, click OK. Marching ants will appear on the image.

3. Click the Save Selection as Channel button at the bottom of the Channels palette to save your selection as a channel.

What's most important is that there is a separation between what you want selected and what you want to protect. If your selection is the opposite of what you want, either Invert the channel (Image > Adjustments > Invert or Command/Ctrl-I) or, if the selection is active, make an inverse of the selection by choosing Select > Inverse or Command/Ctrl-Shift-I.

4. Press Command/Ctrl-4 to view just your alpha channel. In this grayscale view, we can clearly see problems with the mask that don't show up in the marching ants view. We can paint on the alpha channel in this grayscale view to fix the problems.

5. Clean up the mask, starting with the Lasso tool; then use a brush and the Levels command. I used the Lasso to circle the speckly areas and fill them with black or white. I stayed well away from the edges when doing this. With the worst problems fixed, I switched to a hard-edge brush (to avoid introducing any feathering into my mask at this point) and painted out any remaining speckles, again keeping away from the edges. Then I used Levels (Command/Ctrl-L) and moved the black and white input sliders towards the center to make any dark grays in the mask turn to black and any light grays turn to white.

FIGURE 2.25 The channel made from the Color Range selection.

FIGURE 2.26 Using the Lasso tool to select areas and fill them with black or white.

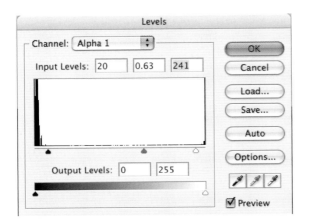

FIGURE 2.27 Using Levels to turn any grays to black or white.

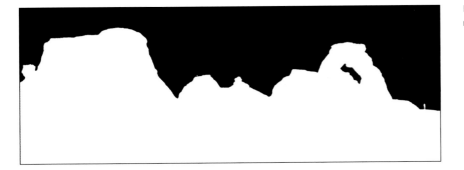

FIGURE 2.28 The cleaned-up mask.

6. When you have cleaned up the alpha channel, return to the composite channel (Command/Ctrl-~) to complete your refinements. Load the alpha channel as a selection by Command/Ctrl-clicking its thumbnail in the Channels palette. To soften the edges, I applied a Gaussian Blur of 0.5 pixels (Filter > Blur > Gaussian Blur). With a good selection, the world is your proverbial oyster. I chose a Curves adjustment layer with which to make a tonal adjustment and then, on a copy of Background layer, I applied sharpening to the selected area.

Selectively Editing with Channels

Channels let you customize settings for selected parts of your image. Here I'll show you techniques to selectively compress an image for the Web using an alpha channel, how to dramatically improve grayscale images, and how to selectively focus an image.

Weighted Optimization Using Alpha Channels

Weighted optimization or regional compression allows you to compress some parts of an image more than others and so get the best of both worlds—good quality in the most important parts of the image as well as a fast download time. Using an alpha channel and the Modify Quality Setting command in the Save for Web dialog box, you choose a compression range between the selected and masked areas of your image. This allows you to preserve detail in the subject while at the same time keeping the your file as lean as possible by reducing detail in the less important areas of the image. However, the practicality of weighted optimization with alpha channels is somewhat diminished by the fact that you have to use high JPEG settings in order to see any benefit. When working with lower quality settings—that is, more compression—weighted optimization can actually make the file size bigger!

A

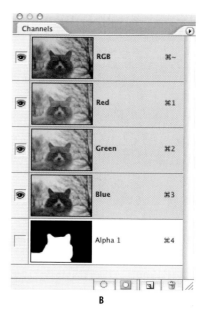

B

FIGURE 2.29 The original image (example **A**) and the Channels palette showing the saved selection (example **B**).

1. Select the part of the image that you want to selectively compress. In the case of the image shown, a general selection with the Lasso tool was sufficient. Save this selection as an alpha channel by clicking the Save Selection as Channel button at the bottom of the Channels palette.

2. Choose File > Save for Web (Command/Ctrl-Option/Alt-Shift-S) and click the 4-Up tab to compare the results of different amounts of compression applied to the image. What you lose in terms of quality you gain in download time.

3. To use an alpha channel to apply varying amounts of compression to the image, click the Modify Quality setting.

NOTE: When using Save for Web to save as a GIF file, you have the option of using an alpha channel to modify the Lossy setting as well as the Dither setting.

FIGURE 2.30 Using my saved alpha channel I varied the amount for compression between 30% (the black or masked areas) and 60% (the white or selected areas).

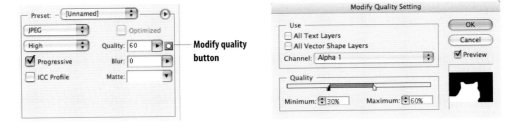

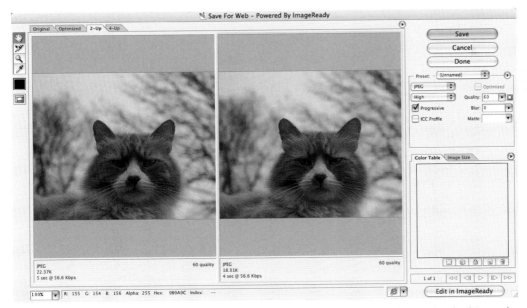

FIGURE 2.31 In the Save for Web dialog box, this 2-Up arrangement shows the difference in file size/download time and quality. The image on the left is compressed without using Modify Quality. The version on the right uses the saved alpha channel to vary the amount of compression applied.

NOTE: You can also apply weighted optimization using a text layer or a shape layer.

4. In the Modify Quality dialog box, choose the alpha channel you created in step 1 from the Channel pull-down menu. Adjust the range of maximum and minimum settings used between the masked area and the selected area. The image sections shown in white will contain the maximum quality areas, and the black sections will contain the minimum. In my case I used a range from 30% to 60%. The resulting file size is smaller and the download time quicker; the trade-off is some degradation of image quality in the background areas.

Converting to Grayscale

NOTE: Note that the alpha channel is not saved with the JPG or GIF file, so make sure you keep copies of your source files.

If your aim is a black-and-white image, either for aesthetic purposes or because you want to print with only a single ink, start with a color image. It may sound contradictory, but for the best quality grayscale image, start with an RGB image. An RGB image contains more data and offers the widest range of options for converting to grayscale. A straight mode conversion (Image > Mode > Grayscale) gets OK results, but rarely better. Like all off-the-rack solutions, sometimes it fits, but often it's a little tight around the collar or a little loose around the shoulder. Add a few simple steps and you can have a dramatically better custom grayscale image. Here are two approaches that use channels. Note that when working with your own files you may want to retain a copy of the file in color.

The Channel Mixer method

The first technique to customize a grayscale image starting with an RGB image is to use the Channel Mixer. The Channel Mixer command lets you choose the percentage of each color channel that makes up the resulting grayscale. This is essentially what Photoshop mode conversion does. The problem is that the Photoshop conversion uses the same percentages for every image: 60% red, 30% green, and 10% blue. The Channel Mixer lets you choose exact percentages of red, green, and blue to make up your monochrome image. This feature does not work with Lab Color images.

1. Open the Greyhound Rock image.

web files

FIGURE 2.32 The original RGB image that we want to convert to grayscale.

2. Before you start mixing channels, evaluate your raw materials. Press Command/Ctrl-1, 2, 3 to look at your Red, Green, and Blue channels. Generally speaking—and it's a very broad generalization—the Red channel will have the most contrast, the Green the most detail, and the Blue the most noise.

3. Return to your composite channel (Command/Ctrl-~) and choose Channel Mixer from the Adjustment Layers pull-down menu at the bottom of the Layers palette. If you've never used adjustment layers, consider this a trailer for Chapter 5, "Adjustment Layers," where they are discussed in detail. In a nutshell, applying the Channel Mixer as an adjustment layer allows you to retain your original layer intact and gives you the flexibility to change your mind about exactly what percentages of Red, Green, and Blue channels go to make up the grayscale.

FIGURE 2.33 The Channel Mixer, where you can experiment with what percentages of Red, Green, and Blue channels will make up your monochrome image.

Channel Mixer

Output Channel: Gray

Source Channels

Red: −7 %

Green: +77 %

Blue: +35 %

Constant: 0 %

☑ Monochrome

OK
Cancel
Load...
Save...
☑ Preview

4. In the Channel Mixer dialog, check the Monochrome checkbox. The Output Channel becomes Gray. Experiment with combining different percentages of your Red, Green, and Blue channels. Typically, the total should add up to 100%—a higher number results in a brighter image and vice versa. Moving the Constant slider will result in an overall brightening or darkening of the image. Usually this is best left alone. Click OK to exit the Channel Mixer.

5. As a last optional step, choose Image > Mode > Grayscale to convert the image to a single channel image. In the dialog that appears, choose Flatten and then click OK. Photoshop will use your channel percentages to make a single-channel document. I'd caution against this unless absolutely necessary—for example, if you are printing in only one of two colors. Once the color information is discarded, it's gone for good, and you never know when you might need it. If you just want your image to look black and white, without officially being black and white, then leave it in RGB.

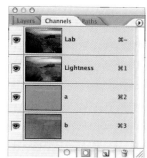

FIGURE 2.34 The color channels in Lab Color mode.

The Lab Color Method

An alternative approach to customizing a grayscale image from an RGB image is to convert it to Lab Color mode and use the Lightness channel. This channel contains all the image detail but very little image noise. Unlike other mode conversions, converting to Lab does not result in loss of image data.

1. Choose Image > Mode > Lab Color, then press Command/Ctrl-1 to view the Lightness channel. When viewing just the Lightness channel, the image will appear grayscale.

2. Next, choose Image > Mode > Grayscale and click OK to convert to Gray-scale mode using the gray values of the Lightness channel.

COMPARING THE GRAYSCALE CONVERSIONS:

FIGURE 2.35 Generic grayscale conversion.

FIGURE 2.36 The Channel Mixer method.

FIGURE 2.37 The Lab Color method.

Selectively Focusing an Image

You can add a lens blur to your image to give selective focus and the effect of a narrower depth of field. Blurring certain areas of your image will accentuate the areas that remain in focus.

The Lens Blur filter uses a depth map to determine what parts of the image are blurred and by how much. This depth map can be based on an alpha channel.

web files

1. Open the Swans image.

FIGURE 2.38 The original image (example **A**) and the result of applying a lens blur based on an alpha channel (example **B**).

A

B

2. Using the Pen tool, start by making a path selection around the neck and head of the central swan. (Alternately, you can make your selection with the Lasso tool.) I've included a saved path with the file. To use the saved path, click on Path 1 in the Paths palette to activate the path.

3. To convert the path (vectors) into a selection (pixels), choose Make Selection from the Paths palette menu. I added a feather radius of 1 pixel.

4. Once you have an active selection, save this selection as an alpha channel by clicking the Save Selection as Channel icon at the bottom of the Channels palette. Press Command/Ctrl-4 to view the resulting channel by itself.

5. With your Gradient tool and your foreground color set to black, use a Foreground to Transparent gradient to blend the bottom of the swan neck into the masked background.

FIGURE 2.39 Draw a Pen path around the area you want to remain in focus.

FIGURE 2.40 Convert the path to a selection. Save the selection and use a gradient on the channel to blend the bottom portion of the mask.

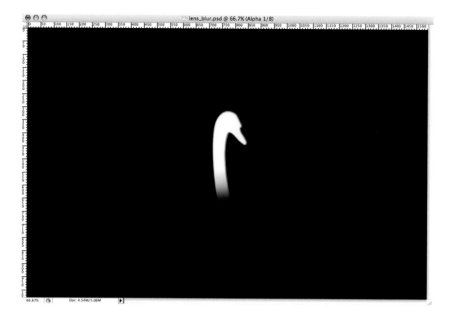

FIGURE 2.40 Convert the path to a selection. Save the selection and use a gradient on the channel to blend the bottom portion of the mask.

6. Return to your composite channel and make a copy of the Background layer as insurance.

7. With the Background Copy layer active, choose Filter > Lens Blur.

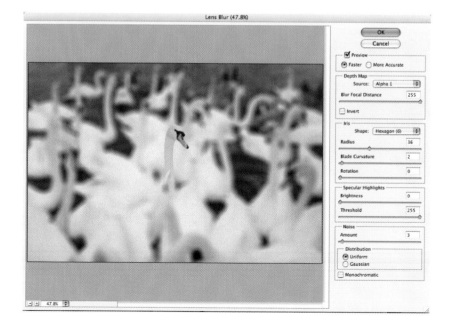

FIGURE 2.41 Lens Blur filter.

8. In the Lens Blur dialog, for Depth Map, choose your saved alpha channel. Check the Invert check box to blur the background rather than the selected swan and drag the Blur Focal Distance slider to the right to determine the amount of blurring. Leave the dialog open.

9. Click the selected swan in the image to identify this as that area you want to remain in focus. This causes the Blur Focal Distance slider to move from 0 to 255 (white).

Make the following adjustments in the Lens Blur dialog:

- Increase the value of Radius slider and watch the background (black area) go out of focus. There's no right or wrong amount—whatever works for you.

- To see the effect of choosing different iris shapes, zoom in close to your preview. The iris shape affects how the image is blurred. Iris shapes are determined by the number of blades they contain. You can change blades of an iris by curving them (making them more circular) or rotating them.

- To make the blurring look more realistic and match any film grain to the focus area, add a small amount of noise. I used the default amount of 3 pixels.

10. Click OK to return to your image.

NOTE: The Faster and More Accurate options affect only how the preview is rendered and not the quality of the result. You might want to switch to More Accurate before committing to the filter, but since Lens Blur is a memory hog, I'd recommend leaving this on Faster.

Creating a Duotone

Duotones are single-channel grayscale images that allow printing an image with custom inks, typically premixed inks from a color matching system such as Pantone. Creating a duotone applies only to offset printing and has no relevance for Web graphics. Duotones allow you to apply a second, third, or fourth color tint throughout your image. Using the Duotone curves you can direct the second or third color to specific tonal ranges in the image, but you can't apply the colors to specific selected areas. By printing in more than one ink, duotones also allow you to extend your tonal range, potentially giving a more tonally rich image than you could achieve with a single color of ink. Technically, an image that uses two inks is a duotone, an image that uses three inks is a tritone, and an image that uses four inks is a quadtone. Photoshop applies the term duotone to all images that are tinted with multiple inks.

Duotones must start out as grayscale images. Because duotones have only one channel, they are very economical in terms of file size.

FIGURE 2.42 The grayscale image (example **A**) and the duotone (example **B**).

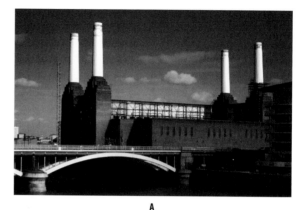

A

B

web files

1. Open the Battersea Power Station image. First, we need to convert it to a grayscale image. Choose Image > Mode > Lab Color, then press Command/Ctrl-1 to view the Lightness Channel. Now choose Image > Mode > Grayscale to convert the image to Grayscale mode using the gray values of the Lightness channel.

2. To convert the grayscale image to a duotone, choose Image > Mode > Duotone. If necessary choose Duotone from the pull-down menu. If duotones seem a little intimidating, you can use one of the preset duotone combos that come with Photoshop. I will almost always use one of these presets as a starting point, probably changing the color, possibly tweaking the curves.

3. In the Duotone Options dialog, click the Load button, choose the Duotones folder, then the Pantone Duotones folder, and choose a preset from the list. Where several options appear that use the same color, 4 uses the least and 1 the most of that color. Click Load to return to the Duotone dialog, where you'll see the chosen second color and its tone curve.

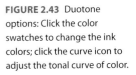

FIGURE 2.43 Duotone options: Click the color swatches to change the ink colors; click the curve icon to adjust the tonal curve of color.

4. To change the color, click the Swatch and you'll be taken to the Pantone solid coated library, where you can type in the number of the color you're after or scroll down the list until you find one you like. Click OK to return to the Duotone dialog.

5. To change the tonal curve, click the curve thumbnail. You can drag the curve up (more ink) or pull it down (less ink), or type in how much ink you want at specific points.

6. When you're done playing with the options, click OK to return to your image.

7. If you are planning to place your duotone image in a page layout program, save the file in Photoshop PDF or Photoshop EPS format.

NOTE: Duotones are more commonly used than tritones or quadtones. While spot color inks are more accurate at reproducing specific colors, practically speaking, if you're going to pay to print in three spot inks then you may as well pay for four process inks, i.e., CMYK, where you can more easily achieve the same effects.

Using Spot Color Channels

Spot color channels are used to apply a spot (custom) color to a selected area or areas of your image for printing. Spot colors are premixed inks used instead of, or in addition to, the process color (CMYK) inks. Each spot color requires its own plate on the press. A varnish also requires a separate plate and is considered a spot color. Like duotones, the technique of using spot colors applies only to offset printing, not to Web graphics.

You use spot colors in the following situations:

- If you can only afford to print in two or three inks.

- If you need to match exactly a color used in a logo.

- If you want to extend the range of a four-color print job by using a "bump plate"—pumping up a particular color so it has more vibrancy than would be possible when printing in CMYK.

- If you want to use a varnish to make specific parts of your design stand out.

Spot colors cannot be applied to individual layers. This means that rather than construct your document with layers, you build the document with spot color channels. These spot color channels overprint the composite image in the order in which they appear in the Channels palette.

This poster by fabulous San Francisco artist Hugh D'Andrade is printed in two colors: black and Pantone 5493.

FIGURE 2.44 The two-color poster (example **A**) and its Layers palette and Channels palette (example **B**).

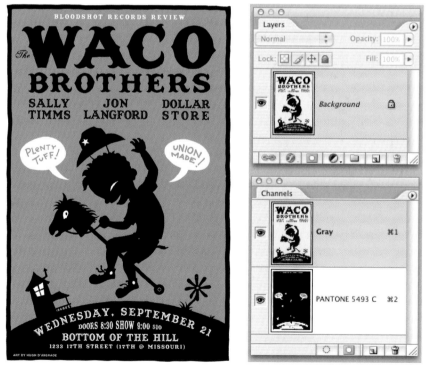

A   B

Note that the Layers palette contains only one layer (and the Layer thumbnail does not show the background color). The Channels palette displays the gray channel—the image is actually in Grayscale mode—which contains all the black information, and the Pantone 5493 channel, which contains the background color.

Here's how Hugh created his artwork:

1. Begin by creating artwork as two separate layers in an RGB document, with the black layer above the background color layer. While this wasn't strictly necessary, Hugh found it easier to do this. To begin with, the gray blue of the background was mixed with RGB colors.

2. When satisfied with the way things look, save a copy of the file in Grayscale mode, choosing Don't Merge to retain the layers.

3. Load the bottom color layer as a selection by Command/Ctrl-clicking its layer thumbnail in the Layers palette, and choose New Spot Channel from the Channels palette menu.

4. Choose the closest Pantone equivalent to the color of the RGB image.

5. For Solidity, leave the value at 0 percent. This option simulates on-screen the density of the printed spot color. A value of 0 percent simulates a transparent ink that completely reveals the inks beneath—in this case black. At a value of 100 percent, the blue gray would completely cover the black.

6. Return to the Layers palette and delete the background layer by dragging its thumbnail to the Trash icon at the bottom of the Layers palette.

7. Select and delete any areas of the spot color channel that need to be knocked out. Because certain details from the Gray channel need to knock out of Pantone 5493 channel—the speech bubbles, the eyes on the boy and the horse—Hugh selected these by Shift-clicking with the Magic Wand tool on the Gray channel and then switched to the Pantone 5493 channel in the Channels palette and deleted these areas.

FIGURE 2.45 The Gray channel (example **A**) and the Spot Color (Pantone 5493) channel (example **B**).

A

B

In Summary

Photoshop features three types of channels: color, alpha, and spot color channels. Color channels tell us a lot about the qualities of our images; alpha channels allow us to save and recall selections and make accurate masks, as well as give us more creative options; and spot color channels expand our range of printing options. It's by using channels that we can understand the images we are editing. As you can see from the examples in this chapter, channels are commonly used in conjunction with other selection methods like paths and layer masks. As we'll see in the next chapter, they are also closely related to, but distinctly different from, layers.

CHAPTER 3

Layers

IF YOU'VE USED PHOTOSHOP FOR MORE THAN 5 MINUTES, you've doubtless had some interaction with layers—even if you didn't know it. These days layers are so fundamental that it's strange to remember they didn't exist in early versions of Photoshop. When Adobe introduced layers in version 3, it was like when silent movies became talkies. A whole missing dimension was added, and we all wondered how on earth we ever managed without them. Layers let us manipulate our images in ways big and small, pedestrian and fantastic. Some things wouldn't be possible without layers, but even those that would, would be a lot harder.

Here's the lowdown:

- Layers let you assign different parts of your composition to different layers so that you can work on one part of an image without disturbing the others. Layers are stacked vertically, and where the layer is transparent or semi-transparent you can see through to the layers below. When there are no layers below, or when those layers are hidden, transparency is represented by a checkerboard pattern.

- By changing the stacking order as well as the attributes of layers, you can change the way different elements of an image overlap and relate to one another.

- As well as the artistic possibilities they offer, layers bring order to what might otherwise be a world of confusion. The breadth and depth of Photoshop's creative options can be overwhelming. Using layer-related features like grouping, Layer Comps, and Smart Objects, we can build our images in ways that are logical, clear, and enable a smooth and efficient workflow.

NOTE: By default, Photoshop displays transparent areas as a checkerboard pattern, distinguishing them from opaque white pixels; you have the option of turning this off in the Transparency & Gamut preferences.

- Experimenting with a layer's opacity and blending mode reveals limitless possibilities for how the colors and tones of one layer interact with those of the layers below it. Blending modes and opacity can sometimes even be used for effortless "selections" by making certain tonal values seemingly disappear.

- Layers allow you to retouch an image nondestructively. By applying your retouching to a separate layer you can retain your original image intact.

- As well as "regular" layers there are special types of layers—adjustment layers, type layers, layer styles—that enhance your range of creative possibilities—see "Layers: A Spotter's Guide" later in this chapter.

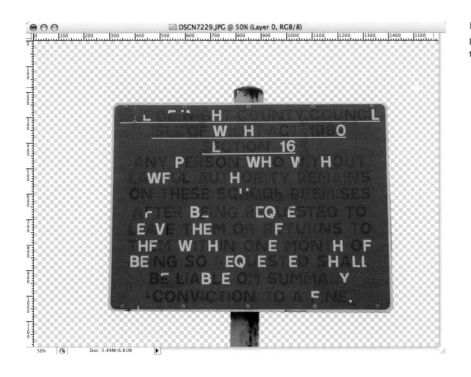

FIGURE 3.01 A checkerboard pattern represents transparency in a layer.

Layers: A Spotter's Guide

Here's a brief description of the different layer types and how to recognize them.

The Background layer is how most Photoshop images begin their life: a single layer, its name italicized. The Background layer differs from other layers in that you can't change its stacking order, its blending mode, or its opacity. However, you can convert a Background to a regular layer by double-clicking its thumbnail and naming it something else. Alternatively, Option/Alt double-click its thumbnail to convert it and leave it named Layer 0. Some people are very protective of their Background layer, and the first thing they do to a file is duplicate it by dragging its thumbnail onto the New Layer icon at the bottom of the Layers palette or by pressing Command/Ctrl-J. That way they can return to the image in its unaltered state and refer to it before and after editing. The downside to this approach is that you immediately double your file size.

Layer groups are folders into which you can put related layers, enabling you to conceptually order your layers as well as keep things neat and tidy. Each group is represented by a folder icon. Click the triangle to the left of the group folder to expand or contract your view of the group contents.

Layer effects allow you to quickly add shadows, glows, bevels, and the like. Layer effects are linked to the layer contents and denoted by an "f" icon to the right of the layer's name in the Layers palette.

Type layers are created automatically when you use the Type tool. The type remains editable and you can add layer effects to your type as well as apply transformations (except Perspective and Distort). If you want to apply filters to your type you must rasterize the type layer, meaning that it is no longer editable as type. A T in the layer thumbnail denotes a Type layer.

Shape layers can by created by using the Pen tool or the Shape tools, which create resolution-independent vector shapes—useful when you need simple graphic shapes with crisp edges. The thumbnail of a Shape layer is shown in your foreground color; the thumbnail of the vector mask attached to the layer indicates the shape.

Type layers and Shape layers contain vector data, that is, crisp type or shapes made up of mathematically defined lines and curves. Because vectors are resolution-independent, they can be scaled to any size and printed at any resolution without losing quality.

Adjustment layers are used to apply color and tonal adjustments in a nondestructive way. Their appearance varies according to what type of adjustment layer you are using. See Chapter 5, "Adjustment Layers," for more information.

Layer masks are like alpha channels, but attached to specific layers. They allow you to determine what parts of a layer are shown and what parts are masked or hidden. Layer masks are the subject of Chapter 4.

Clipping masks allow you to restrict the influence of specific layers. Typically a layer affects everything that is below it in the layer stack. Using a clipping mask, layers can be clipped by a base layer so that the clipped layers affect only that base layer. The thumbnails of clipped layers are indented with a right-angle arrow pointing to the layer below.

Smart Object layers are embedded files that maintain a link to the original data, which means you can nondestructively transform their content. You can make multiple copies of a single Smart Object and it will be updated when one of the copies is edited—just like the concept of Symbols in Adobe Illustrator or Macromedia Flash, and similar to the concept of style sheets in page layout programs. You can still apply layer styles and adjustment layers to the individual Smart Objects without affecting all copies, so you're not in any way restricted. Smart Objects are identified by an icon in the bottom right corner of their layer thumbnail.

About the Layers Palette

Mission Control is the Layers palette, where you can show and hide layers, create new layers, and work with groups of layers. The Layers palette menu contains additional commands and options.

Choose Palette Options to change the size of the layer thumbnail as well as how that thumbnail is displayed. If you have lots of layers, you might consider turning off thumbnails to improve performance and save monitor space, relying on the layer names to identify each layer. Entire Document displays the contents of the entire document; Layer Bounds shows only the thumbnail to the object's pixels on the layer.

FIGURE 3.02 A layered composition (example **A**), and its associated Layers palette (example **B**).

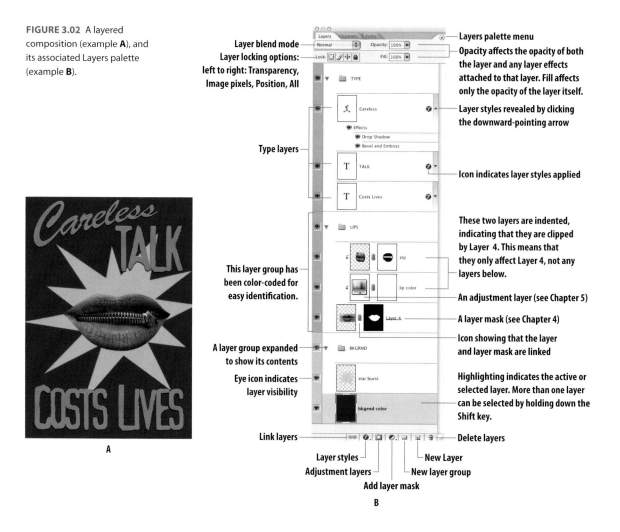

A

B

Layer blend mode

Layer locking options: left to right: Transparency, Image pixels, Position, All

Type layers

This layer group has been color-coded for easy identification.

A layer group expanded to show its contents

Eye icon indicates layer visibility

Link layers

Layer styles

Adjustment layers

Add layer mask

Layers palette menu

Opacity affects the opacity of both the layer and any layer effects attached to that layer. Fill affects only the opacity of the layer itself.

Layer styles revealed by clicking the downward-pointing arrow

Icon indicates layer styles applied

These two layers are indented, indicating that they are clipped by Layer 4. This means that they only affect Layer 4, not any layers below.

An adjustment layer (see Chapter 5)

A layer mask (see Chapter 4)

Icon showing that the layer and layer mask are linked

Highlighting indicates the active or selected layer. More than one layer can be selected by holding down the Shift key.

Delete layers

New Layer

New layer group

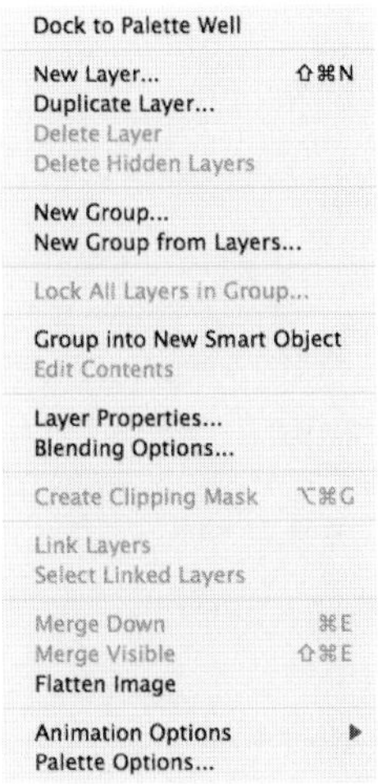

A

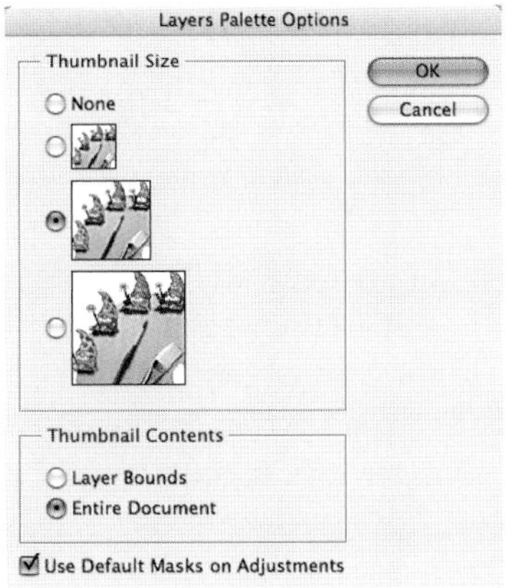

B

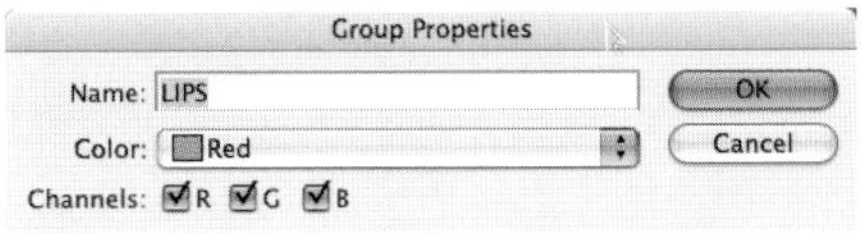

C

FIGURE 3.03 The Layer palette menu (example **A**) and Palette options (example **B**). Note the layer groups can be color-coded to roughly correspond with the color of the layer content (example **C**).

Selecting and Moving Layers

To select a layer, click on its thumbnail. This highlights its name and causes it to appear in the title bar of the document window. The more layers you have the more you need to be mindful of managing those layers, which is not a big deal, but it's common to get confused about which layer you have selected. So if you're not getting the results you expect, take a step back and check the Layers palette to make sure you're on the correct layer.

To change the layer order, drag the layer thumbnail up or down in the Layers palette. Alternatively, use the Arrange options under the Layer menu to bring a layer to the top or send it to the bottom of a layer stack, or move it one level up or down, or reverse the layer stacking order.

Some tasks, like painting or applying filters, can only be applied to one layer at a time. However, transformations like moving, rotating, scaling, or applying styles from the Styles palette, can be applied to multiple layers at once. To select multiple layers, select the bottommost layer and then Shift-click to select the topmost layer; or to select noncontiguous layers, Command/Ctrl-click their thumbnails. As well as being able to select multiple layers, you can also link layers by selecting multiple layers and then clicking the link icon at the bottom of the Layers palette. The difference is that linked layers stay linked when you change the selection in the Layers palette. Linking layers maintains the relationship between the layers so that if you transform one layer the other layers that are linked to it are similarly transformed. Because you can Shift-click to select multiple layers in CS2, linking is less necessary than before.

FIGURE 3.04 Temporarily unlinking a layer by Shift-clicking its linking icon.

To temporarily unlink one layer from the rest, Shift-click its link icon to the right of the layer thumbnail and a red X appears on top of layer's link icon. To relink the layer to the others, Shift-click on the red X and it disappears, leaving the link icon intact.

In a multilayered document it's often convenient to select layers with the Move tool, rather than hunting and pecking on the Layers palette. If you have selected Auto Select Layer (or Auto Select Group) in the Options bar, you can click in the document on the layer content you want to select and the layer containing pixels under the cursor is selected. Because it's easy to forget you have Auto Select checked and mistakenly move layers around, I prefer to leave this unchecked and instead Command/Ctrl-click with the Move tool on the image to get the same result. When using the Move tool you can also Ctrl/Right-click on your image to access a contextual menu of all the layers below the position of your cursor.

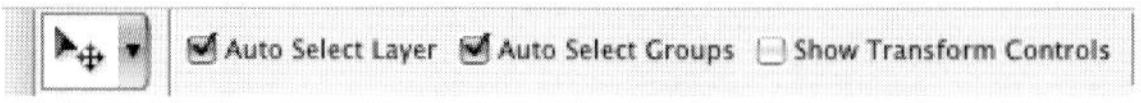

FIGURE 3.05 The Auto Select layer option for the Move tool.

FIGURE 3.06 Ctrl-clicking or right-clicking on the image brings up a menu of layers beneath the pointer.

To select everything on a particular layer, Command/Ctrl-click on the layer thumbnail. As you Command/Ctrl-click, hold down the Shift key to add to an active selection or the Option/Alt key to subtract from an active selection. If the layer has a layer mask attached to it, Command/Ctrl-click the layer mask thumbnail instead.

FIGURE 3.07 Load a layer's pixels as a selection by Command/Ctrl-clicking the layer thumbnail, or if there is a layer mask attached to the layer, by Command/Ctrl-clicking the layer mask thumbnail.

Use the Move tool to reposition selected layers in the composition. For incremental moves use the arrow keys to nudge the objects by 1 pixel, or by 10 pixels if you hold down the Shift key. Note that if you have a selection active, only that part will move.

Showing and Hiding Layers

You can turn layers on and off to find out what content is on what layer and also to evaluate how a particular composition looks with or without a given layer. Click the Eye icon next to a layer, the layer group, or layer effect to show or hide its content. If you want to display just that layer or group, Option/Alt-click the Eye icon. Or you can drag through the Eye column to change the visibility of multiple items in the Layers palette. A layer prints only if it is visible. If a layer is within a group, click the triangle to the left of the Folder icon to expand the group. Option/Alt-click the triangle to open or close a group and the groups nested within it.

Adding Layers to Your Document

There are a variety of ways to create layers:

- Paste a selection, create type, or create a shape to create a new layer automatically.

- Click the New Layer button in the Layers palette. The new layer appears above the selected layer; if you want the new layer to be added below the currently selected layer, you can Command/Ctrl-click the New Layer button or New Group button in the Layers palette—or you can drag it to wherever you want it go in the layer stack.

- Drag one image onto another. As you do so, hold down the Shift key to register the layers (if the source and destination images have the same pixel dimensions) or to the center of the document window (if the destination image has a different pixel dimensions). To drag multiple layers from one image to another, first select those layers in the Layers palette and drag to the destination document. If you want a merged copy of the layers you are dragging, choose Select All, then Edit > Copy Merged (Command/Ctrl-Shift-C), then in the destination document choose Edit > Paste.

- Copy or cut a selection from an existing layer to a new layer. With an active selection choose either Layer > New > Layer Via Copy to copy the selection into a new layer or Layer > New > Layer Via Cut to cut the selection and paste it into a new layer.

A

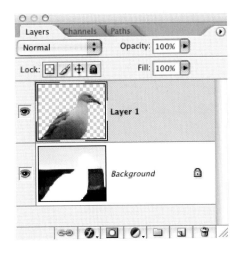

B

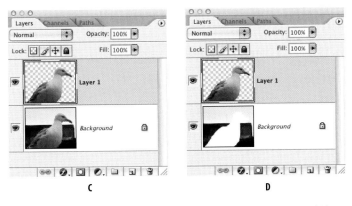

C   D

FIGURE 3.08 Making new layers from an active selection (examples **A** and **B**). Layer Via Copy copies your active selection to a new layer (example **C**). Layer Via Cut makes a new layer of your selection, leaving a hole on the original layer filled with transparency or the background color if the layer you are cutting from is a Background layer (example **D**).

Managing Layers

Layers are easy to manage, but a little housekeeping will maximize your productivity.

Layers and File Size

When working with layers the news is nearly all good, but there are a few things to keep in mind. As you work on an image keep an eye on its file size at the bottom of the application window. The first number indicates the flattened document file size—i.e., if all the image data were compressed into a single layer. The second number indicates the document size, taking into account additional layers, alpha channels, and paths. Specifically, these numbers refer to the size of the document in memory. Depending on the file format chosen the actual file size on disk may be considerably smaller.

FIGURE 3.09 Keep an eye on your document file size as you add layers.

Layers add to a file's size, although it's worth noting that only the active pixels of a layer are taken into account—the surrounding transparent areas don't cost you anything. Still, too many layers can bloat a file as well as clutter things up, so delete any you no longer need by dragging their thumbnails to the Trash icon at the bottom of the Layers palette.

There is no right number of layers. How many you have is determined by the demands of your image and your available computer memory, but most of all by common sense. Keep it simple, but don't think twice about adding layers as needed.

Flattening Layers

Only some file formats preserve layers: Photoshop, TIFF, Photoshop PDF, and Large Document. If saving to a format that doesn't support layers, you need to flatten the image. Flattening compresses all layers into a single background layer, making any transparent areas white. Flattening reduces file size, but you lose the advantages that layers offer. When switching color modes, for example from RGB to CMYK, be sure to click Don't Flatten or Don't Merge to preserve your layers. Note that color mode conversions will affect adjustment layers, either flattening them into the image, or discarding them altogether. See Chapter 5, "Adjustment Layers."

When the Selection button is checked, your selection is previewed in the Color Range dialog box like a grayscale alpha channel. While I've never found any reason to change this, you can, if you wish, see your selection preview in the image window and choose from the Selection Preview drop down menu to view the selection as Grayscale, against a black or white matte, or as a Quick Mask.

Certain types of image usage necessitate flattening your image. However, if you choose File > Save As you can make a flattened copy and retain your layered original. When creating Web images in JPEG or GIF formats, use the Save for Web option under the File menu to create a flattened copy rather than overwriting your layered original. In the relative scheme of things, disk space is cheap and time is tight, so I always keep layered versions of my images; that way if I need to make edits I can call up the layered original and save a new flattened version from that. It used to be necessary to flatten files before importing them into a page layout program, but this is no longer the case with the most recent versions of InDesign and QuarkXPress.

Layered files are flexible; flattened files are not, so think carefully about flattening.

Merging Layers

Merging is like flattening, but on a local level—only your visible or your select layers are flattened into a single layer. Merging allows you to combine elements that no longer need to be on separate layers, cutting down on file size and clutter. When you merge layers, what's on the top layers replaces the overlapped data on layers below. The intersection of all transparent areas in the merged layers remains transparent. Merging layers permanently changes layers, so don't be too zealous with your spring cleaning.

A more cautious approach is to merge layers *and* keep the separate layers. This does nothing to reduce file size, but can speed up workflow while an image is in an unfinished state by creating a work-in-progress layer. Merging selected layers is also useful when you need to apply a filter, like Unsharp Mask or Smart Sharpen, to the whole image rather than individual layers.

To merge multiple layers into a new layer and still keep your existing layers, select the layers you want to merge and press Command/Ctrl-Shift-Option/Alt-E. The new layer is added over the topmost selected layer.

FIGURE 3.10 A merged work-in-progress layer.

As an alternative to merging layers, you can make the layers into a Smart Object layer. That way you can work with the original separate layers, if necessary, by editing the Smart Object. For more information, see "Nondestructive Editing with Smart Objects" later in this chapter.

Naming Layers

It only takes a moment and it can save confusion later down the road. Double-click the layer or group name in the Layers palette, and enter a new name. You can also color-code layers to establish relationships that are easy to identify. Use a consistent naming convention for your layers. For example, I name sharpened layers "Sharp 150/1/0;" the first number records the amount of sharpening, the second the radius, and the third the threshold.

Grouping Layers

Using layer groups shortens the list of names on the palette and means less scrolling up and down trying to find the layer you're after. You can expand and contract the group folder as necessary by clicking the arrow to the right of the group name.

You can nest groups within other groups up to five levels deep. You can also move, rotate, scale, duplicate, lock and unlock, hide and show, link, and copy the contents of layers grouped together.

To group layers, select the layers you want to group and choose New Group from Layers in the Layers palette menu. Once the group is created you can add layers to it by dragging them to the group folder. You can mask multiple layers by applying a layer mask or vector mask to a group rather than an individual layer. See "Viewing and Editing Layer Masks" in Chapter 4, "Layer Masks." To ungroup the layers, select the group and choose Layer > Ungroup Layers.

FIGURE 3.11 Using layer groups was essential for creating this type poster (example **A**). Each letter is on its own layer and is in a group folder that also contains any associated retouching layers and adjustment layers (example **B**). The ordering of the layer groups began as alphabetical, but I found it necessary to change the layer stacking order to have certain letters overlap with others.

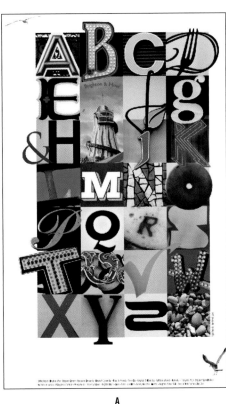

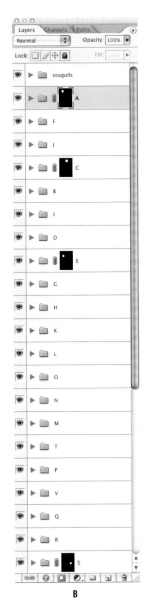

A

B

Aligning and Distributing Layers

The Align and Distribute buttons are straightforward, but can be confusing nonetheless. I sometimes find it takes a few clicks to get exactly what I want. To align or distribute layers, you use either the menu options (Layer > Align or Layer > Distribute) or the button in the Move tool options bar. If you have a selection active, your layer(s) are aligned relative to that selection. Choose Command/Ctrl-A to select all if you want to align your selected layers to the whole canvas. Note that you also have several nonprinting visual aids available under the View menu—Guides, Grid, and Smart Guides (guides that appear automatically)—to help you when manually aligning and distributing layers.

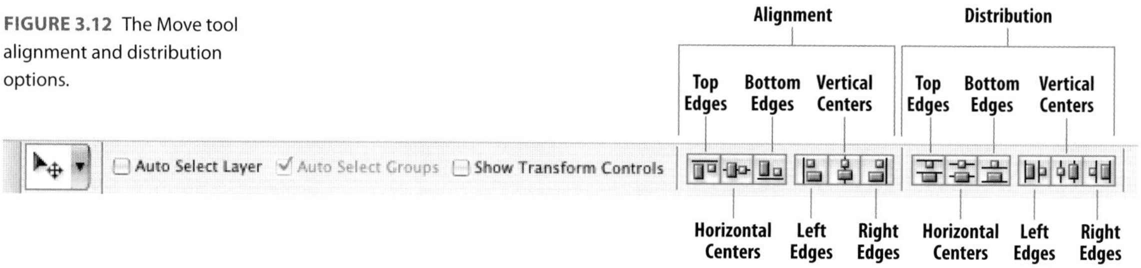

FIGURE 3.12 The Move tool alignment and distribution options.

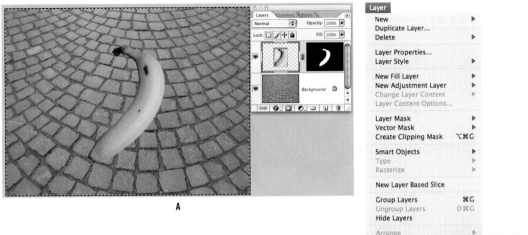

FIGURE 3.13 Centering a layer within the canvas by aligning to a selection (examples **A** and **B**). Distributing and aligning layers (examples **C** and **D**). First, I chose Command/Ctrl-A to select the whole canvas, and then I distributed the horizontal centers and aligned the vertical centers.

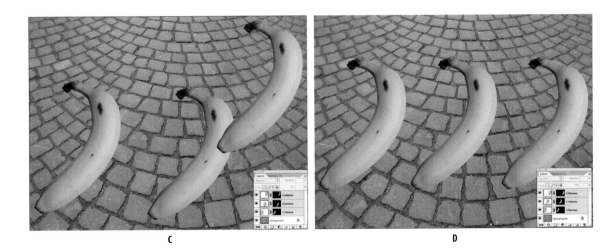

Locking Layers

You can lock a layer's transparency, its pixels, and its position to protect it from change. When you're finished with a layer you can lock it fully. Or, while you're still working on the layer, you may want to lock only its transparency to prevent "painting outside the lines," but still allow repositioning of that layer. Or vice versa. When a layer is fully locked, a solid lock icon appears to the right of the layer name. When a layer is partially locked, the lock icon is hollow. For Type layers, Lock Transparency and Lock Image Pixels are always on.

NOTE: If a layer has a layer mask attached and the transparency of that layer is not locked, you can paint on the transparent areas but you won't see any paint unless you discard or disable the layer mask.

To lock all layer properties, click the Lock All icon at the top of the Layers palette (shown in Figure 3.02).

To partially lock a layer, select one or more of these lock options:

- **Lock Transparency** restricts editing to the opaque areas of the layer. Semitransparent pixels are restricted to their transparency level, i.e., painting with a 100% opacity brush on an area of 20% opaque pixels yields only a 20% opaque result.

- **Lock Image Pixels** prevents modification of the layer using the painting tools.

- **Lock Position** prevents the layer from being moved. Note that Background layers are locked by default.

FIGURE 3.14 Locking Transparency. Painting without locking transparency (example **A**) and with the transparency locked (example **B**). Note the Lock icon next to the layer name in the Layers palette.

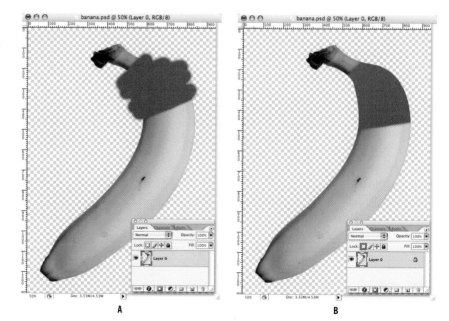

A   B

Rasterizing Layers

Certain elements of a layered composition may be made up of vectors: for example, type layers, shape layers, or Smart Objects containing vector data. Vectors lend themselves to crisp artwork and have the advantage of being resolution-independent, but while they remain as such you can't use your painting tools or filters on these layers. There may be times (though perhaps not as often as you may think) when you need to rasterize a vector layer—that is, convert it to pixels. When you do so, a warning dialog informs you that you'll no longer be able to edit the layer as vectors. Select the layers you want to rasterize (Layer > Rasterize) and then choose the appropriate option from the submenu.

Working with Layer Styles

Layer styles are effects like drop shadows, bevels, and glows that you can add to a layer with a single click. These effects change with the content of the layer and can be updated at any time. Layer styles fit in with our approach of nondestructive editing because while the effects are attached to a specific layer, they do not actually change the pixels of the layer. To access layer styles, double-click the layer thumbnail. Layer styles are identified with an "f" icon to the right of the layer's name in the Layers palette. Clicking the triangle next to the f shows the list of layer styles applied to that layer.

Layer styles are best demonstrated on a simple piece of text, but can be applied to anything. The following examples show the effects applied individually, using the default settings for each one. It's when effects are combined and their options carefully tweaked that they become unique.

FIGURE 3.15 The Layer Styles menu in the Layers palette.

FIGURE 3.16 The Normal text and the same piece of text with layer styles applied.

The original text.

Drop Shadow

Inner Shadow

Outer Glow

Inner Glow

Bevel and Emboss

Bevel and Emboss with Contour

Bevel and Emboss with Texture (wood)

Satin

Color Overlay

Gradient Overlay

Pattern Overlay (wood)

Stroke

Here are some tips for working with layer styles:

- Because layer styles are so easy to apply, they can look generic. Avoid this minor pitfall by editing your layer effects and applying them in combination.

- Once you have combined various layer effects to create a look you like, save it as a custom style, which then appears in the Styles palette and can be applied with a single click. In the Layers palette, select the layer with the style that you want to save as a preset and drag it into the Styles palette or onto the New Item button in the Styles palette.

- Layer effects such as Drop Shadow, Inner Shadow, Outer Glow, Inner Glow, Bevel and Emboss, and Stroke work on the edges of your layer and are most effective on layers with transparency. If your layer fills the whole canvas, the style will have little or no effect.

- The Satin, Color Overlay, Gradient Overlay, and Pattern Overlay effects can be used on opaque and transparent layers.

- Using Contour lets you control the edge style of the effect.

- To copy a layer style from one layer to another, Option/Alt-drag the layer effect to another layer.

- To give the appearance of a common light source shining on the image, check Use Global Light in the Layer Style dialog box.

- Don't know what angle to use? With the Layer Styles dialog open, check Drop Shadow and then move your cursor onto your image (it changes to the Move tool). Click and drag to determine the angle of the shadow as well as the distance.

- To scale a layer effect without scaling the layer itself, choose Layer > Layer Style > Scale Effects.

- Sometimes you want more control than layer styles allow. In such cases you can convert a layer style to an image layer and then edit the layer as normal. For example, to cast a drop shadow, begin with a Drop Shadow layer style, convert the layer style to an independent layer, then use your transformation tools to distort the shadow. (See "Creating a Cast Shadow" later in this chapter for an example of this technique.) The downsides are that the layer style is no longer officially a layer style and won't update as you change the original image layer, and also that, depending on how complex your layer style, the resulting layer(s) may not be able to replicate it with complete accuracy—see Figure 3.17.

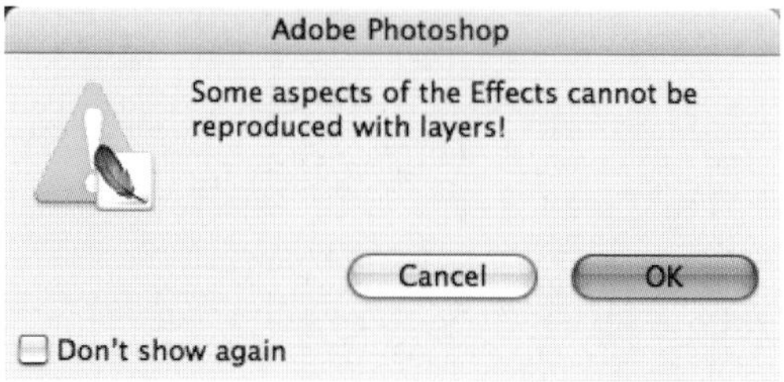

FIGURE 3.17 When creating a separate layer from layer styles, the result will approximate your layer styles—with varying degrees of success.

The Land of Happy Accidents: Layer Blending Modes and Opacity

With blending modes you commonly arrive at fantastic results that are unexpected and unintentional. One of the great things about using layer blending modes and opacity sliders is that there's no penalty for experimentation. Blending mode and opacity changes are nondestructive so you can experiment to your heart's content without harming your image data. I will give definitions for what the different blending modes do, but it's a lot easier just to experiment. The possible combinations are infinite, which can be overwhelming. The good news is there are no rules. If it looks good, then it is good (and vice versa). Before we look at the layer blending modes, let's take a quick look at layer opacity and why there are two sliders.

- Opacity affects the layer and its layer effect if there is one.

- Fill opacity only affects the layer transparency, leaving the layer effect unchanged.

When you are in the Move tool you can quickly change the opacity of a selected layer by using your number keys: 1 for 10%, 5 for 50%, 63 for 63%, etc. For 100% opacity press 0.

FIGURES 3.18 Layer opacity. The opacity and fill opacity at 100% (example **A**). The opacity at 50%; note both the type layer and the layer effect (drop shadow) are both affected (example **B**). The opacity at 100% and the Fill Opacity at 0% (example **C**); note the type is affected but the shadow remains at 100%.

Using Blending Modes

A layer's blending mode determines how its pixels blend with the pixels of any underlying layers. Combined with layer opacity, blending modes can be used to create myriad special effects. To give an idea of what's possible I've created a simple composition of a red rectangle on top of an image of the Grand Canyon and applied various blending modes to the red rectangle layer, all with an opacity of 100%. I've omitted showing blending modes that in some contexts have no effect, and those that, also in some contexts, differ from each other indistinguishably.

FIGURE 3.19 Layer blending modes.

The original image

The Blend Mode menu

Multiply

Screen

Soft Light

Difference

Hue)

Saturation

Color

Luminosity

Using blending modes involves a certain amount of trial and error and serendipity. It's all about trying them. This book cover mock-up shows how applying blending modes to various color rectangles transforms an otherwise generic picture of the Golden Gate Bridge into something unique.

FIGURE 3.20 Everyone who's ever been to San Francisco has this exact picture of the Golden Gate Bridge (example **A**). Placing an overlapping rectangle of color on separate layers (example **B**) and then experimenting with the blending modes of those layers helps to spice it up (example **C**).

A

B

C

Darkening Blending Modes: Multiply, Darken, Color Burn, and Linear Burn

Any of these blending modes produces a darker image. For my money Multiply is the most useful, and is the blending mode I use the most for compositing images, dropping out white or high-contrast details, and fixing overexposure.

Multiplying any color with black produces black and multiplying any color with white leaves the color unchanged, making this blending mode invaluable for compositing images with handwriting or line drawing when you want the white areas to drop out. See Figure 3.21.

A

B

FIGURE 3.21 The poem and the poppies are on separate layers (example **A**); choosing Multiply as the blending mode for the poem makes the paper drop out (example **B**).

Multiply can also come to the rescue with exposure problems. A quick fix for an overexposed image is to make a copy of the layer and set the blending mode of the copy to Multiply, building tonal and color density in the too-light areas. If the effect is too strong, reduce the opacity of the copied layer; if it's not strong enough, make another copy.

A

B

FIGURE 3.22 Fixing overexposed images. The original overexposed image (example **A**). The result of copying the background layer and setting its blending mode to Multiply with an opacity of 70% (example **B**).

Darken uses the base or blend color—whichever is darker—as the result color; working with a duplicate layer where the pixels are the same has no effect.

Color Burn darkens and saturates.

Linear Burn darkens the base color by decreasing the brightness.

Lightening Blending Modes: Screen, Lighten, Color Dodge, Linear Dodge

This group of blending modes does the opposite of the correspondingly named blending modes in the previous group, with Screen being the opposite of Multiply. Where Multiply can be used to fix overexposure, Screen can be used to fix underexposure.

I find Screen to be by far the most useful of the lightening blending modes. In the earlier example of the handwritten poem, to make the text white instead of black, we can invert the layer (Image > Adjustments > Invert or Command/Ctrl-I) and set the blending mode to Screen.

FIGURE 3.23 The text turns white when the layer is inverted and the blending mode set to Screen.

Because the black pixels of the blending layer have no effect on the layer below, using Screen is also an easy way to "select" subjects on a black background, like fireworks. If necessary, you can build density by duplicating the screened layer.

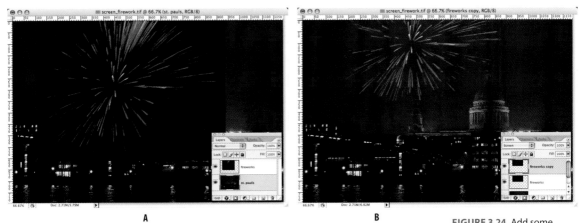

A   B

FIGURE 3.24 Add some fireworks (example **A**). The result of changing the blending mode to screen, scaling, repositioning, and duplicating the Fireworks layer to build color density (example **B**).

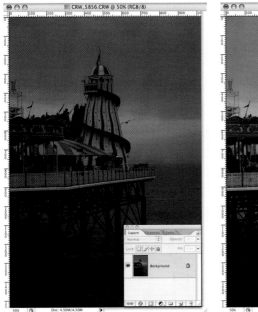

A   B

FIGURE 3.25 The original underexposed image (example **A**). The result of copying the background layer and setting its blending mode to Screen with an opacity of 70% (example **B**).

Contrast Blending Modes

These blending modes increase contrast. The Overlay mode either screens or multiplies colors, depending on the color of the pixels on the layer below, which means it makes darks darker and brights brighter, resulting in increased contrast. Overlay is useful when retouching images—see "Dodging and Burning an Image" later in this chapter.

Like Overlay, Hard Light increases contrast but the results are stronger, whereas using Soft Light gives a more subtle result. Vivid Light, Linear Light, Pin Light, and Hard Mix are seldom useful, but try them, you never know...

Color Blending Modes

These blending modes affect the hue, saturation, or tonality of an image. Or to put it another way, they affect the color, the intensity of color, or the degree of lightness and darkness of an image.

Hue changes the hue of the underlying image, but not the tonality or saturation.

Saturation changes the saturation of the underlying image, but not the hue or tonality.

Color affects the hue and saturation of the underlying image but not the tonality. Of this group Color is the heavy hitter and can be used to colorize images. While there are many ways to colorize Grayscale images (after you've converted them to RGB) or historic photos (see the following illustration), using layers and the Color blending mode is arguably the most intuitive. (See Chapter 5, "Adjustment Layers," for another approach to colorizing a photo.)

Add layers as necessary, making their blending mode Color; then choose an appropriate foreground color and paint in that color with any of your painting tools.

If necessary, use the selection tools to limit areas where the paint goes.

Experiment with varying the layers' opacity as well as with the color.

To quickly change the color of the paint on a layer, lock the transparency of that layer, select a new foreground color and press Option/Alt-Delete. Alternatively, you can press Option/Alt-Shift-Delete without having to first lock the layer transparency.

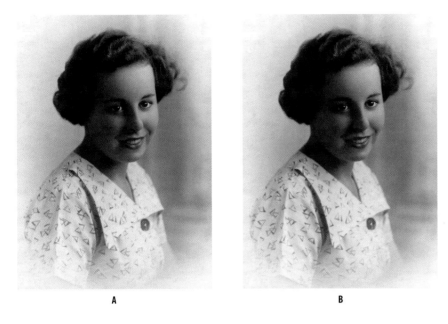

A   B

FIGURE 3.26 I colorized this family photograph (example **A**) by painting on layers in the Color blending mode and varying the opacity of those layers (examples **B** and **C**).

C

Luminosity affects the tonality of the underlying image, but not the hue or saturation. This is useful when using adjustment layers to make tonal changes to an image when you don't want to introduce any color shifts. For an example of using this blending mode, see "Adjustment Layers: Reasons to Be Cheerful" in Chapter 5, "Adjustment Layers."

Layer groups have an additional blending mode, Pass Through. This is the default blending mode for layer groups and means that the group has no blending properties of its own—any adjustment layer, blending modes, or opacity changes applied to a group affect the way that group interacts with the layers below. Choosing a blending mode other than Pass Through means that the layers in the group are blended together first and then that composite group is blended with the rest of the image using the selected blending mode.

FIGURE 3.27 Layer groups and blending modes. The blending mode of Group 1 is set to Pass Through, affecting the gap layer beneath (example **A**). The blending mode of Group 1 is set to Normal so that blending modes and opacity changes are restricted to the layers within the group (example **B**). In both examples, the blending modes of the "danger" and "no parking" layers are set to Multiply.

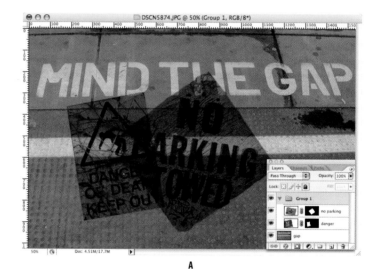

A

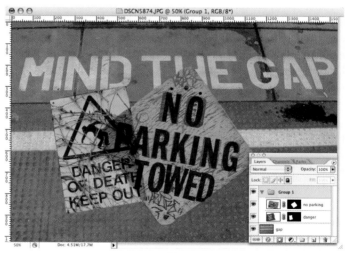

B

Comparative Blending Modes

These blending modes are used to compare one layer to another:

Exclusion results in a color solarization effect—handy if you're in a psychedelic frame of mind, but not much use otherwise. Black pixels have no effect on the underlying image; white pixels invert the underlying image; and grays partially invert depending on their brightness.

Difference lets you compare two images that look the same so you can spot the difference. For example, you know that one of the two versions of the same image has retouching applied, but you don't know where. Shift-drag one image on top of the other and change the blending mode of the top layer to Difference. All pixels that are the same will be black; any differences show up as nonblack pixels. Difference also has a rather esoteric but occasionally useful role in determining neutral grays when color-correcting images. See "Color Correction by the Numbers" in Chapter 5, "Adjustment Layers."

Blending Mode Shortcuts

If you're doing a lot of work with blending modes it's worth committing these to memory:

If you're in the Move tool press Shift-+ (plus sign) to move up through the list of blending modes and Shift--(minus) to move down through the list. Alternatively, press Shift-Option/Alt plus the relevant letter to switch to the blending mode:

Normal	N	Color Dodge	D	Hard Mix	L
Dissolve	I	Linear Dodge	W	Difference	E
Darken	K	Overlay	O	Exclusion	X
Multiply	M	Soft Light	F	Hue	U
Color Burn	B	Hard Light	H	Saturation	T
Linear Burn	A	Vivid Light	V	Color	C
Lighten	G	Linear Light	J	Luminosity	Y
Screen	S	Pin Light	Z		

NOTE: Switching color modes, for example, from RGB to CMYK, you may experience color shifts where you have applied blending modes. You can minimize this by making a copy of your RGB image (Image > Duplicate), then flattening this file before you convert to CMYK.

Using Custom Blending Options

The Blending options in the Layer Styles dialog box let you control which pixels in the current layer stay visible and which pixels from the underlying layer show through the current layer. For example, you can drop out the blue pixels of the active layer or allow the red pixels from underlying layers to show through. Theoretically this means you can mask a layer based exclusively on the brightness of its pixels without having to dirty your hands making selections that define your mask by area.

However, while it's fun to mess around with these options, I've never found much use for them. Masking "by the numbers" works only on specific types of images, those with distinct areas of pure colors. For example, dropping out blue might work fine if your sky is a pure blue and is the only blue in the image; if not, the effect is reminiscent of an early 1980s pop video, dropping not only the blues you don't want, but also those you do.

You can refine the effect by holding down your Option/Alt key to split the sliders and define a range of partially blended pixels. But conventional layer masking techniques still give you more control. Furthermore, because the Layers palette doesn't show changes to layers made by using Blend If sliders, this approach is not as transparent (pun intended) as using layer masks, which we discuss in Chapter 4.

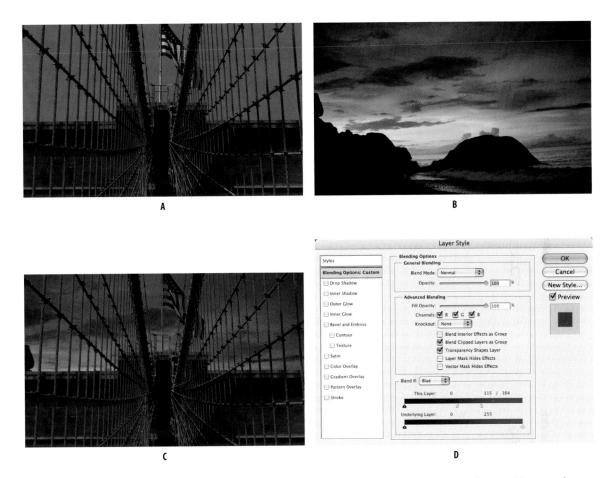

FIGURE 3.28 Using the Blend If sliders to drop out the blue sky in the Brooklyn Bridge image (example **A**) and so reveal the sunset from the image below (example **B**). In the result shown (example **C**), the white slider has been dragged to the left and divided by holding down the Option/Alt key. This is effective in dropping out the sky, but unfortunately we also lose some of the flag. For the Brooklyn Bridge layer, blue pixels with a brightness value of 0-114 are shown; those with a value of between 115 and 164 are partially blended, and those with a value of between 165 and 255 are hidden (example **D**).

Experimenting with Multiple Compositions Using Layer Comps

Layer Comps is a great productivity tool. A snapshot of the state of your Layers palette, a layer comp lets you experiment with multiple versions of a layout in a single document, saving time and disk space, but most importantly freeing you from worrying about what layer went with what on which version, and what its exact opacity and blending mode were.

A layer comp remembers the following layer options:

- Layer visibility—whether a layer is shown or hidden.

- Layer position in the document.

- Layer appearance—whether a layer style is applied to the layer and the layer's opacity and blending mode.

To create a layer comp, choose Window > Layer Comps to display the Layer Comps palette, and click the Create New Layer Comp button at the bottom of the Layer Comps palette. The new comp reflects the current state of layers in the Layers palette. You can add descriptive comments in the Layer Comp dialog box that appears and decide which options apply to the layers: Visibility, Position, and Appearance.

To view a layer comp at any time, click the icon to the left of its name in the Layer Comps palette. A layer comp can't restore some actions, such as deleting or merging a layer, converting a layer to a background, or converting to another color mode. In such instances, a caution icon appears next to the layer comp name. You can either update the comp by clicking on the Update Layer Comp button at the bottom of the palette to capture these changes as a new state, or choose Clear to remove the alert icon and leave the remaining layers unchanged.

FIGURE 3.29 In the Layer Comp Options dialog box, choose what you want the layer comp to remember.

FIGURE 3.30 Using Layer Comps, I mocked up three versions of this book cover. Each layer comp remembers the visibility and position of the layers, their opacity and blending, and any layer effects applied.

If you want to send your layer comps to a client, you can export them to separate files or to a Web Photo Gallery. Choose File > Scripts and then choose one of the following:

NOTE: In InDesign and Illustrator, you can access and choose layer comps that have been saved with a Photoshop (psd) file.

- **Layer Comps To Files** makes an individual file for each layer comp.

- **Layer Comps To PDF** exports all layer comps to a PDF file, with one page for each layer comp.

- **Layer Comps To WPG** exports all layer comps to a Web photo gallery.

Layer Compositing Strategies

First, a couple of logistical issues:

- For best results when combining images, use images with the same or similar pixel dimensions.

- Preferably use images in the same color mode. If they are in different color modes, the image you are copying will be converted to the color mode of the destination image. For example, dragging a CMYK image to an RGB image converts the CMYK image to RGB. The resulting conversion may be satisfactory, but if you want more control you'll need to handle the mode conversions yourself before compositing.

What strategy should you follow when compositing images? Should you assemble all your source images into one master document and make edits to the individual layers within that master layered document? Or should you work on the source images as independent files before collecting them into a master document?

Both approaches have pros and cons; I often end up using a combination of the two. On one hand, it's not until you see all the images together in one document that you really know how they will interact—and consequently what you need to do to them. On the other hand, combining all images in one document can result in a monster-sized document with a lot of redundant information.

To simplify the process and to clarify your thinking, I suggest that you begin every project with a pencil sketch. Using Adobe Bridge, view the thumbnails of all the files you have short-listed for your project. Consider making a Contact Sheet for use as a visual reference. From within Bridge, select the files you want to include and then choose Tools > Photoshop > Contact Sheet II. Referring to the contact sheet, sketch as many different compositions as you can think of, experimenting with the scale and placement of the different elements. Don't skip this step; no matter how rough or embarrassing your sketches, they help you to quickly evaluate whether certain ideas are worth pursuing. Once you have a clearer idea of where you're going with your composition, then you can crop your source images accordingly. There's no point in working with image data that you're certain you don't need.

I would suggest doing any masking in the master document, but if you have already masked the individual images using a layer mask, the layer mask will travel with the image when you drag it into the master document.

Nondestructive Editing with Smart Objects

Smart Objects are the latest development in the evolution of Photoshop layers. Working with pixel-based media, we are inhibited by the rules of resolution. Photoshop allows us to stretch and scale our images as if they were Silly Putty, but if we take too many liberties, we irrevocably damage our images. Not anymore. Smart Objects let us scale, rotate, and warp layers nondestructively and without resampling the resolution, because we are working on a proxy or preview of the original file, rather than the file itself.

Smart Objects—identified with an icon in the bottom right corner of their layer thumbnail—are essentially child files embedded in the original parent document. For example, a Smart Object can be Adobe Illustrator artwork or it can be made up from two or more Photoshop layers. The Smart Object keeps a link to the source data inside your Photoshop document. What you work on is a layer that contains a composite of that data. Any changes to a Smart Object's opacity or blending mode affect the appearance of the Smart Object layer, not the original embedded file. When you edit a Smart Object (Layer > Smart Object > Edit Contents), the Smart Object opens in its native application, or—if the Smart Object was made from Photoshop layers—in a separate Photoshop document containing the individual layers. When you modify the source document, Photoshop updates the Smart Object—or objects if there's more than one instance of the same object—in the parent document.

To create a Smart Object, either choose File > Place to import artwork, drag and drop or copy and paste from Illustrator into your Photoshop document.

You can also convert one or more layers into a Smart Object. This is like merging layers but without giving up the flexibility of keeping individual image elements on separate layers—otherwise known as having your cake and eating it too. Select two or more layers, and from the Layers palette menu choose Group Into New Smart Object. Thereafter, if you double-click the Smart Object layer to edit the Smart Object, a separate document opens with the Smart Object elements unmerged on individual layers. When you edit, save, and close the file, your main document updates to reflect your edits, similar to the way linked files work in a page layout application.

NOTE: When copying and pasting or dragging and dropping artwork from Illustrator, make sure that both PDF and AICB (No Transparency Support) are enabled in the File Handling & Clipboard preferences of Adobe Illustrator.

FIGURE 3.31 The original Web button—vector art from Illustrator—placed, duplicated, and distributed (examples **A** and **B**). The button replaced with an alternative version (example **C**).

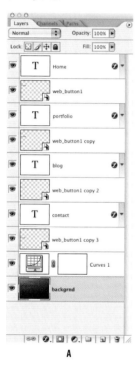

A

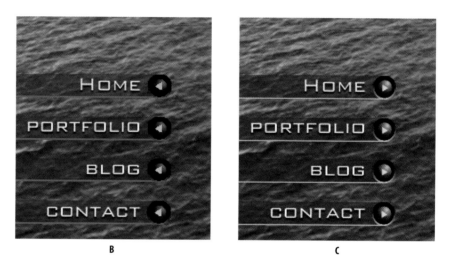

B　　　　　C

If you duplicate an existing Smart Object, all instances are updated when you replace or update one instance of the Smart Object. For example, in this Web navigation bar, I placed a Web button from Illustrator as a Smart Object. I duplicated its layer three times and used Distribute to evenly space the buttons. I later decided I didn't like the buttons, so I selected any one of their layers and chose Layer > Smart Objects > Replace Contents. I picked an alternative button and clicked Place. All instances of the button were replaced with the new button.

If, on the other hand, you are working with multiple versions of the same Smart Object and don't want all instances to be linked to a single original, choose Layer > Smart Objects > New Smart Object via Copy rather than duplicating the Smart Object layers. That way the new Smart Object will be independent.

Now here's something to blow your mind: you can place a Camera RAW file as a Smart Object. Typically when you open a Camera RAW file you rasterize a working copy, discarding potentially useful data if you want to readjust the image exposure further on down the line. But in placing your Camera RAW file (and you should definitely be using this format if your digital camera supports it), not only can you scale and rescale the file as much as you want (so long as you don't exceed the maximum noninterpolated file size in the Camera RAW dialog), but if you double-click the Smart Object thumbnail you are returned to the Camera RAW dialog where you can continue to "re-expose the image." It takes the concept of nondestructive editing to new heights.

So, you may be thinking, are Smart Objects too good to be true? Well, yes. You can't paint on or apply filters to Smart Objects without first rasterizing them—undermining the benefits of their being Smart Objects. You can, however, use clipping masks to apply color to them. See the second step in the following section, "Creating a Layer Sandwich." Also, while you can add a layer mask to a Smart Object, you can't link a layer mask to a Smart Object. This means that as soon as you move the Smart Object layer, it becomes disassociated from its layer mask. Thankfully, there's a workaround: make the Smart Object into a group and then apply the layer mask to the group. Before you move the Smart Object, select the group in the Layers palette rather than the Smart Object thumbnail. I expect this issue will be resolved in the next version of Photoshop.

In the following illustration I placed each of these Camera RAW images as a Smart Object so that I could experiment with the scaling of the different elements without worrying about degrading the image quality. When I'm finished, Photoshop re-renders the image from the parent files. The Layers palette shows each image in its own group so that I can apply layer masks to the group as a workaround, because Smart Objects don't allow scaling of layer masks with the Smart Object layer.

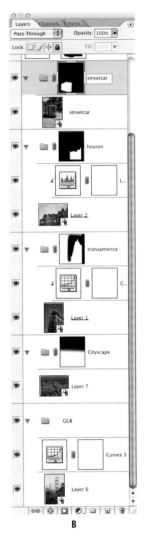

A

FIGURE 3.32 This composition (example **A**) converted the different elements to Smart Objects so that they could be scaled separately. The Layers palette (example **B**) shows each image in its own group, a workaround to apply layer masks.

Useful Layer Techniques

In the step-by-step examples that follow, I'll show you some practical layer techniques, the kind of stuff that is bread and butter to a Photoshop artisan. Let's begin with an easy one.

Extending an Image

Often you wish that the edge of an image extended farther—perhaps because you want to put type or other image elements over this area or you want the image to conform to the aspect ratio of your page. Using layers, it's a cinch to extend one or more sides of an image, so long as the area you're trying to extend doesn't contain significant detail and you're not trying to extend it too much. This technique breaks the rules. It involves upsampling and distorting a portion of the image, two things that are definitely not kosher because they diminish image integrity and resolution. However, if you'll indulge me in a cliché (and it wouldn't be the first time), you can't make an omelet without breaking eggs.

web files

1. Open the Mazatlan image.

A

B

FIGURE 3.33 The original image (example **A**) and the image with the foreground extended (example **B**).

2. Convert the Background layer into a normal layer so that when you increase the canvas size in step 3 the added area will be transparent rather than opaque. Option/Alt-double-click the Background layer thumbnail.

3. Increase the canvas size to give the image expansion room by choosing Image > Canvas Size (Command/Ctrl-Option/Alt-C). In this instance, we want to add canvas at the bottom of the image so click the top center proxy square to indicate the position of the existing image within the new canvas size. I increased the height of the image from 3.41 inches to 4 inches. You can also express this dimension as a percentage, which is sometimes useful. Click OK.

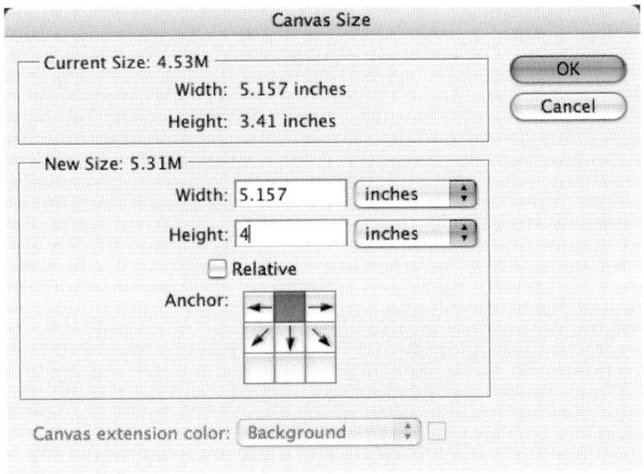

FIGURE 3.34 Adding extra canvas to the bottom of the image.

4. Make a marquee selection of the foreground area, making sure you drag from one edge of you canvas to the other. This area is going to be stretched to fill the empty canvas at the bottom of the image. The bigger the selection the better, but avoid any areas of detail that will be adversely affected by the stretching.

5. Copy this selection to a new layer by pressing Command/Ctrl-J or choosing Layer > New > Layer via Copy.

FIGURE 3.35 A marquee selection of the area (example **A**) that will be copied to a new layer (example **B**) and then stretched using Free Transform (example **C**).

6. Select the copied layer, and using Free Transform (Command/Ctrl-T or Edit > Free Transform), pull down from the bottom center handle to stretch this layer to the bottom of the image canvas.

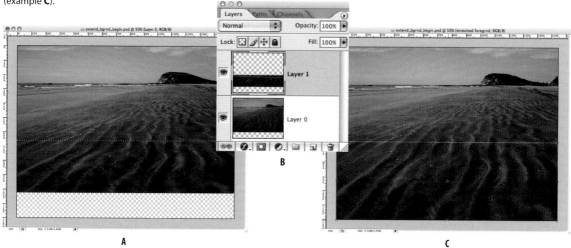

A

B

C

Creating a Layer Sandwich

Here's a super simple, super-effective technique you see all the time used on magazine mastheads, but it's applicable any time you want to sandwich one layer between two parts of an image. Figure 3.36 shows the finished version.

FIGURE 3.36 The finished image with the elk head overlapping the magazine "masthead.

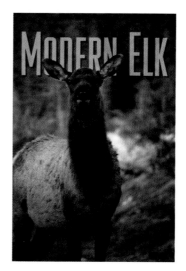

Starting out with my elk image, I placed the Modern Elk masthead (an Illustrator file) as a vector Smart Object. That way I can resize the masthead as necessary without degrading its quality. The masthead now sits on top of the elk's head.

FIGURE 3.37 The masthead placed as a Smart Object.

This step isn't strictly necessary, but I include it here to make a point about Smart Objects. I can't fill my masthead with another color because it is a Smart Object. However, I can create a new layer above the masthead, fill that layer with a color and then choose Layer > Create Clipping Mask or Command/Ctrl-Option/Alt-G so that the color is visible only in the type areas. For more on clipping masks, see "Masking with Transparency" in Chapter 4, "Layer Masks."

FIGURE 3.38 Putting a color fill layer above the masthead and making it into a clipping mask to affect the color of the Smart Object.

1. Select the elk layer and make a selection of the head. I used the Pen tool and then converted the path to a selection, but the Magnetic Lasso is also a good choice. With the selection active I press Command/Ctrl-J (or Layer>New>Layer via Copy) to copy it to a new layer.

FIGURE 3. 39 A selection of the elk head copied to a new layer.

2. Drag the copied layer above the masthead, and there you have it: a layer sandwich.

FIGURE 3.40 The copied layer dragged above the masthead in the layer stacking order.

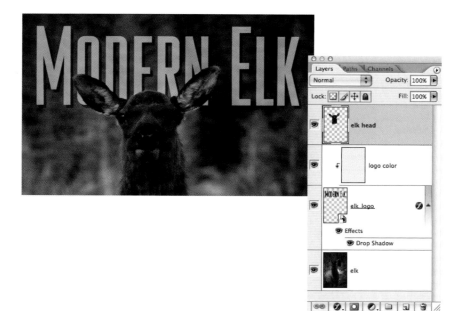

Creating a Cast Shadow

There are several variations on this technique, but the basic principles are these: Start with a Drop Shadow layer style, make it into an independent layer, and then distort it and adjust its opacity to your liking.

1. Open the Clown image.

web files

A   B

FIGURE 3.41 The finished image with a cast shadow (example **A**) and our starting point (example **B**).

2. Mask the clown as the first step in Making a Shadow. To save time, I've included a saved alpha channel with this file. To load it as a selection, Command/Ctrl-click on the Clown alpha channel thumbnail in the Channels palette. To use this selection as a layer mask, select the Clown layer and then click on the Add layer mask icon at the bottom of the Layers palette (third one from the left).

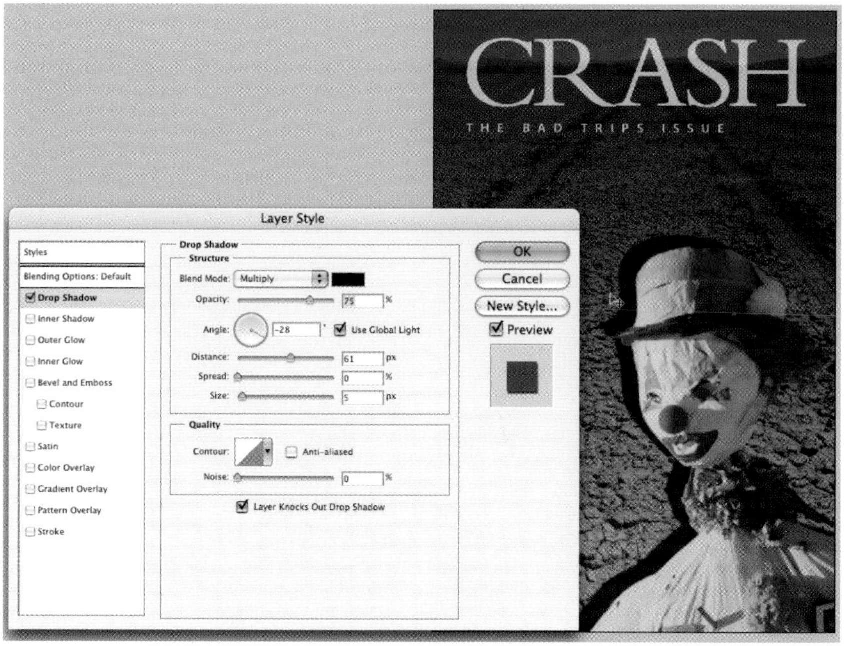

FIGURE 3.42 The clown, masked with a layer mask.

3. Add a basic drop shadow as a starting point by either double-clicking the Clown layer thumbnail or selecting Drop Shadow from the Layer Effects icon at the bottom of the Layers palette—the one with the "f" on it. Click the Drop Shadow check box in the list on the left. Because this shadow shape is only a starting point, it's not necessary to set options. In other contexts, it might be useful to move your pointer into the image area and drag to position the shadow relative to the layer. Click OK.

4. To control the shadow shape, choose Layer > Layer Style > Create Layer. This puts the shadow on its own layer, which is no longer attached to the Clown layer.

5. Select the Clown's Drop Shadow layer, choose Free Transform (Command/Ctrl-T) and holding down the Command/Ctrl key to distort the shape, pull the shadow to cast it over the clown's right shoulder—or wherever you like.

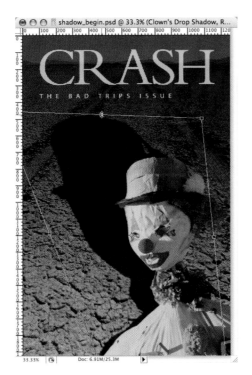

FIGURE 3.43 Transforming the shadow layer.

6. To make the density of the shadow less uniform, lock the transparency of the shadow layer, press D to restore your foreground and background colors to their default black and white, and paint with a Foreground to Background Gradient across the shadow shape. I dragged from bottom right to top left so that the shadow dissipates as it gets farther from the subject. You may need to try this a few times before you get a result you want. If you go wrong, press Command/Ctrl-Z to undo and try again.

FIGURE 3.44 Painting over the shadow with a black-to-white gradient.

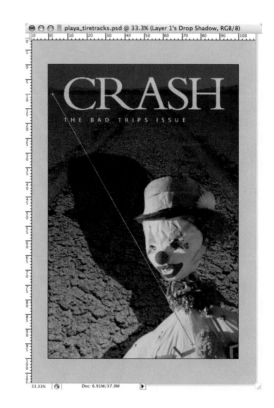

7. Adjust the opacity of the shadow layer to your liking.

8. Optionally, blur the shadow more by choosing Filter > Blur > Gaussian Blur.

9. To distort the shadow shape, either try Edit > Free Transform > Warp or using the Liquify filter—you'll need to unlock the layer's transparency for this to work. I used Liquify (Filter > Liquify or Command/Ctrl-Shift-X) and painted over some of the edges with the Forward Warp tool, the default tool, at the top left of the Liquify tool palette. I selected Show Backdrop (bottom right) to see shadow layer in the context of the whole composition.

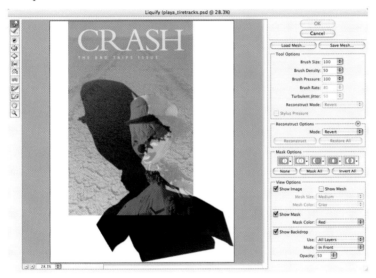

FIGURE 3.45 Distorting the shadow shape using the Liquify filter.

Adding a Reflection

A complementary technique to casting a shadow is adding a reflection. You can use pretty much any image to try this out.

In the example shown (Figure 3.46), I increased the canvas height to 200%. Next, I duplicated the layer, moved it into position, flipped it vertically, and reduced its opacity to 75%. To make the house look as if it were reflected on water, I specifically avoided the Ripple and the Ocean Ripple filters, which tend to look fake. Instead, I used an image of water (it's a good idea to build your own library of textures), which I put on a layer above the upside-down house and then experimented with its opacity (I used Luminosity 78%). I cloned over the seam where the two houses meet using the Clone Stamp tool to give the impression of a riverbank. To clone from one layer and paint the cloned pixels to another I checked Sample all layers in the Clone Stamp options. Finally, I used the Liquify filter on the reflected layer (as in Step 8 in the "Creating a Cast Shadow" example) to make sure that the reflection didn't look like an exact duplicate of the house.

FIGURE 3.46 A cast reflection (example **A**) and the file's layer palette (example **B**) showing how the image is constructed.

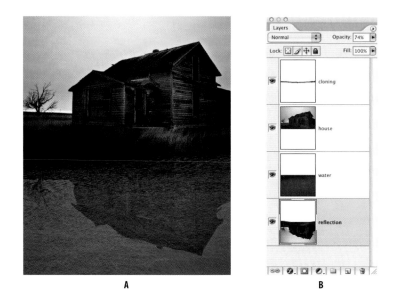

A

B

Converting an Image to Line Art

There are various techniques for doing this, but this is possibly the simplest and works well with images that have well-defined contours and contrast.

web files

1. Open the Worthing Pier image.

FIGURE 3.47 The original image (example **A**) and the finished line art version (example **B**).

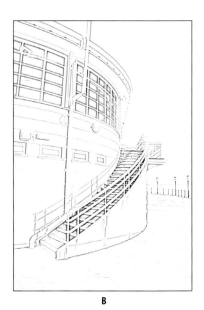

A

B

2. Duplicate the layer (Command/Ctrl-J) and then choose Image > Adjustments > Desaturate (Command/Ctrl-Shift-U) to Desaturate the new layer.

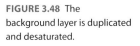

FIGURE 3.48 The background layer is duplicated and desaturated.

FIGURE 3.49 A duplicate of the desaturated layer is inverted (example **A**), its blending mode converted to Color Dodge, and a Gaussian Blur applied (example **B**).

3. Duplicate the desaturated layer and then choose Image > Adjustments > Invert to invert the layer. Switch the blending mode of the inverted layer to Color Dodge (this will cause the layer to turn white), and then apply a Gaussian Blur filter to the layer. The higher the radius the more gray values you introduce into your line art—I chose a radius of 15.

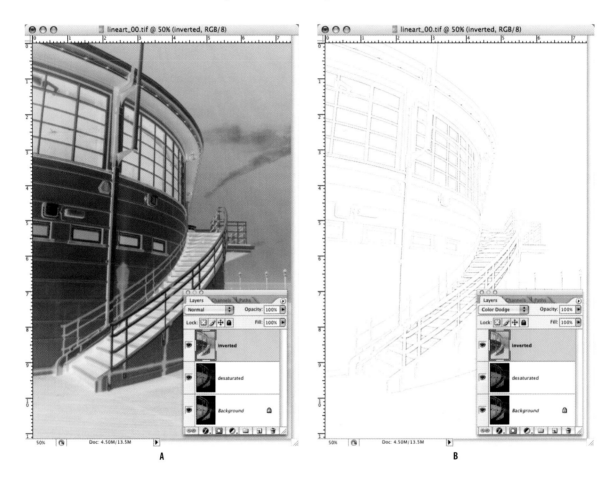

A   B

4. As an optional final step you may need to increase the contrast of the image. Merge your three layers—hold down Option/Alt-Shift and choose Merge Visible from the Layers palette. If you want to preserve your background layer, make a duplicate of it first. Increase the contrast on this layer by choosing Image > Adjustments > Levels and moving the black and white input sliders towards each other.

Adding Film Grain

Adding noise to all or part of a composition can effectively disguise differences in image characteristics. The Add Noise filter simulates film grain and can be used either to help blend in retouched areas or just to create a different visual mood. However, the Add Noise filter is destructive—add too much noise and there's no way to remove it—except by blurring, which creates as many problems as it solves. Using layers with the Overlay blending mode, we can add the noise to a separate layer without harming the original image.

In the example shown I've replaced the flat sky of the original image with a more expressive sky. The original image was shot on ISO 400 slide film and is consequently quite grainy; the new sky is a digital image shot at ISO 100 with no discernible grain. So I need to add some grain to the new sky.

A

FIGURE 3.50 The finished composition (example **A**). The original image and the replacement sky (examples **B** and **C**). Because the sky is a digital image, it lacks the grain in the sign image, shot on slide film.

B   **C**

web files

1. Open the layered image, "Fresh Cream." This is a composition in progress, with a new sky layer visible in the Layers palette.

2. Create a new, empty layer above the sky layer and name the layer Noise.

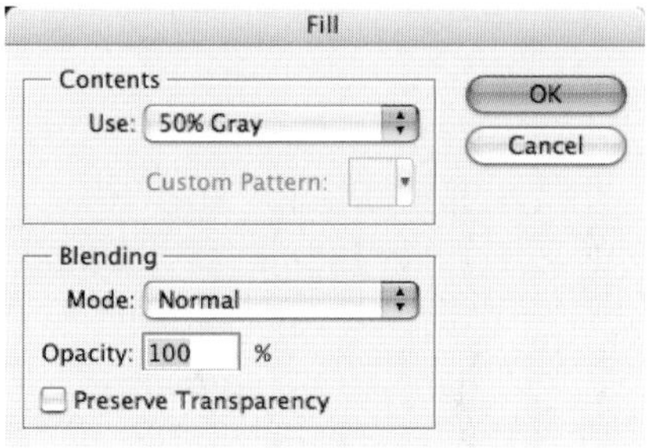

FIGURE 3.51 To apply noise nondestructively, fill a layer with neutral gray, change its blending mode to Overlay, and then apply the noise to that layer rather than to the image itself.

3. Fill the layer with neutral gray (Edit > Fill, and from the pull down menu choose 50% Gray), because the Add Noise filter needs some pixels to work with.

4. Change the blending mode of the Noise layer to Overlay. Here's the trick with the Overlay blending mode: as I mentioned in "Contrast Blend Modes" earlier in the chapter, Overlay makes the darks darker and the lights lighter. And it leaves the neutrals unaffected. The Noise layer now becomes invisible until we apply the next step.

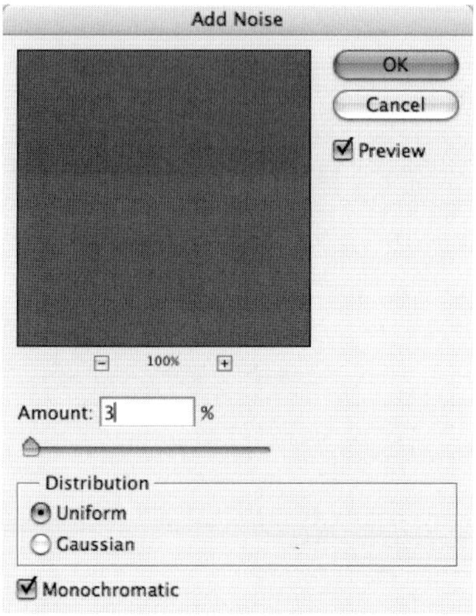

FIGURE 3.52 The Add Noise filter.

5. Choose Filter > Noise > Add Noise. I chose Uniform noise with an amount of 3%. The filter adds a grain that also adds contrast because half of it is darker than 50% and half is lighter, and the noise now shows up in the sky, making it more closely match the structure of the rest of the image. The effect is subtle, but clearly discernible on zooming in.

FIGURE 3.53 A close-up of the sky before (example **A**) and after (example **B**) the noise is applied.

A   B

In this example we added noise to an Overlay layer; you can use this technique to add any kind of texture to your image in a nondestructive way. Here's an example of applying different filters to a neutral gray layer set to Overlay mode and experimenting with the opacity of that later:

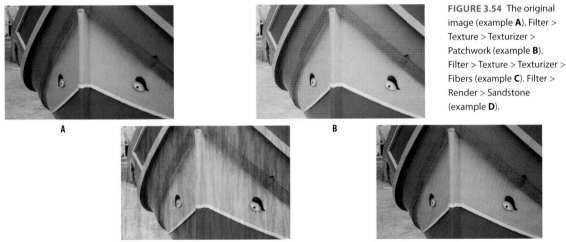

A

B

C

D

FIGURE 3.54 The original image (example **A**). Filter > Texture > Texturizer > Patchwork (example **B**). Filter > Texture > Texturizer > Fibers (example **C**). Filter > Render > Sandstone (example **D**).

Dodging and Burning an Image

Here's another use of the Overlay blending mode that works on the same principle as the previous example. The Tool palette features Dodge and Burn tools that respectively lighten or darken areas of an image. But there's a better, nondestructive way of getting the same result. Apply dodging and burning to a separate layer using the Overlay blending mode. Here's how.

web files

1. Open the Nathalian image.

A   B

FIGURE 3.55 In example **A**, the subject's face is in shadow and the highlights in the background are too strong. In example **B**, I've used a dodge and burn layer to "dodge" the shadows on the face and "burn" some of the background highlights.

2. Create a new layer above the Background layer and name it Dodge and Burn.

3. Fill this layer with neutral Gray (Edit > Fill, and choose 50% Gray from the Use pull-down menu).

4. At the top of the Layers palette, change the blending mode of the Dodge and Burn layer to Overlay. The Overlay blending mode ignores neutral gray pixels.

5. Make white your foreground color. Choose a soft-edge brush and an opacity of around 25%, and "dodge" the shadows on the face. Change your brush size and opacity as necessary. Be careful not to go too far when dodging deep shadows because this reveals unsightly noise in these areas and may look fake. When you're satisfied with the result, switch your foreground color to black and "burn" any highlights in the background that are distracting. If the highlights are blown out, that is, if the RGB values in the highlight read 255, 255, 255 on your Info palette, the burning will have no effect.

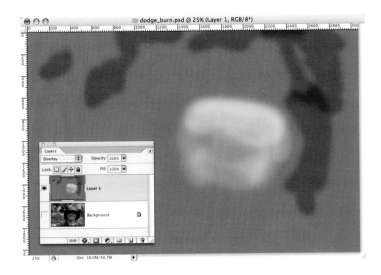

FIGURE 3.56 The Dodge and Burn layer viewed by itself: Where the pixels are darker than 50% gray the subject is darkened; pixels lighter than 50% lighten, and neutral gray has no effect.

Retouching on a Separate Layer

Layers play a valuable role when combined with Photoshop's retouching tools: They let you add retouching elements to a separate layer and keep your original image intact. Without such an approach, if an error to your retouching is outside your number of history states, your image may be permanently damaged, or at best, require a lot of work to fix the error. Retouching on a separate layer lets you view just that layer to see exactly where the retouching has been applied, and delete or soften as needed any retouching that isn't working, or just trash the whole layer and start again if things are beyond redemption.

Of the major retouching tools—the Healing Brush, Spot Healing Brush, Patch tool, and Clone Stamp—all but the Patch tool give you a Sample All Layers option so that you can simultaneously clone from one layer or more layers and paint to another. (Even when using the Patch tool, you can get around this shortcoming by first copying the area you are patching to a separate layer using Layer via Copy (Command/Ctrl-J).

Let's see how retouching on a separate layer works in practice with the Healing Brush tool. When the Healing Brush samples, it analyzes the texture, color, and luminosity of the source area. Unlike the Clone Stamp, which literally duplicates the clone source and paints it over the original information, the Healing Brush merges the texture from the sample area into the color and luminosity of the destination area.

1. Open any image of a person with wrinkles around the eyes.

FIGURE 3.57 The original, unretouched image.

2. Create a new layer above the Background layer and name it Retouching.

3. Choose the Healing Brush tool. In the tool options, make sure that Source is set to Sampled, and that Aligned and Sample All Layers are both checked.

FIGURE 3.58 The Healing Brush options.

Source: ● Sampled ○ Pattern: ▼ | ☑ Aligned ☑ Sample All Layers

4. Zoom in so that you can comfortably see the wrinkles around the eyes. The Healing Brush adds a 10–12-pixel spread to the brush, so start with a brush hardness of about 75% and a brush size of 30 pixels. Option/Alt-click a short distance from a wrinkle line to sample the "good" pixels, and then reposition your pointer over the wrinkle and paint. For best results, make many short strokes rather than long sweeping ones. Don't try to cover too much ground with one stroke. Also, avoid frequently resampling the source area as you may be accustomed to doing with the Clone Stamp tool. When working near edges where there is a transition in color or texture—for example, at the edge of the face in this image—it's helpful to first make a selection of the area you are healing. A selection helps you avoid sampling colors from outside the area. If you go wrong, choose the Eraser tool to paint away any retouching lines you don't want. Just for kicks (and sometimes this can be helpful), view the retouching layer by itself.

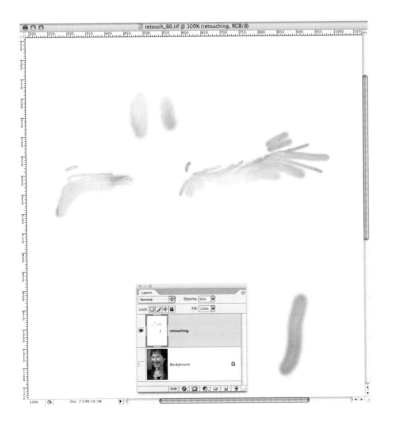

FIGURE 3.59 Viewing just the Retouching layer.

5. Once you have applied the retouching, soften the effect by reducing the opacity of the retouching layer. After all, wrinkles add character, and we don't want people to look as if they've been ironed.

FIGURE 3.60 The result of the retouching layer set to 100% opacity (example **A**) and 60% (example **B**).

In Summary

The concept of layers is integral to Photoshop. Layers allow you to composite images quickly, safely, and efficiently as well as provide an unprecedented range of creative possibilities through the combining of layer styles, blending modes, and opacity options. The more sophisticated aspects of layers—like grouping, layer comps, layer effects, and Smart Objects—enhance your workflow and reduce any organizational confusion that comes from working with multiple layers. But there's even more that layers can do. We'll see in the next two chapters that layer masks and adjustment layers make a great thing even better.

CHAPTER 4

Layer Masks

WHATEVER THE PROBLEM, layer masks are probably part of the solution. Layer masks are so versatile, you can use them for all kinds of creative and workaday Photoshop tasks, from making a cutout to put in a page layout application, to blending textures for unique backgrounds, to making seamless composites from a collection of images, to stitching together landscape panoramas. In this chapter we'll learn how layer masks work, how easy they are to use, and how effective they can be when editing your images.

What makes layer masks so essential is that they allow you to work nondestructively—a point I'll return to repeatedly. Here is mantra number 1: Mask it, don't delete it. Layer masks let you change your mind as often as you like without messing up your image. Masking, rather than deleting parts of a layer means that no pixels are harmed. If you go wrong, or just want to experiment with other solutions, you can restore the layer to the way it was. In effect, you have an infinite number of undos that are saved with your file, unlike with the History palette, where your limited number of History States are lost every time you close the file.

FIGURE 4.1 Choose an image. Make a selection. Turn the selection into a layer mask. Bob's your uncle.

But, despite their ease of use, some people avoid layer masks and insist on doing things the hard way: adding unnecessary layers that bloat the file and make it cumbersome to work with, or—worse—deleting backgrounds, only to find later that they need, but are unable, to retrieve the lost information.

TOM ERIKSON

Click here to turn a selection into a layer mask.

I have a confession: the first time I became aware of layer masks, I avoided them. Consequently, I have several legacy images that I'd love to modify and improve upon, but which are effectively uneditable. For example, I made this family collage when Photoshop version 3 was released as a way of learning how to use layers. Unfortunately, I didn't have the brain space to simultaneously grasp the potential of layer masks. I deleted images from their backgrounds, making it next to impossible to experiment with different positioning of the individual images and, since the images were removed from their backgrounds, robbing me of the chance to seamlessly blend the layers together with layer masks. Layer masks maximize our options when working on images. It's a win-win situation: layer masks give you more creative freedom and, because you are masking, not deleting, you can recover from your less successful explorations.

FIGURE 4.2 Because the individual backgrounds have been deleted rather than masked, changing the position of any of the layers is made significantly more difficult.

Maybe it's the name that's off-putting: two big concepts—layers and masks—rolled into one. Really, a layer mask is nothing more than a channel—which itself is nothing more than a saved selection—attached to a specific layer. A layer mask functions like an old-fashioned stencil, masking—or protecting—selected areas of an image, leaving the areas that have been cut out open to modification.

Now for mantra number 2: Black conceals, white reveals. To modify a layer mask and affect how much of its layer is concealed or revealed, you paint or fill in either black or white. Painting in black conceals; painting in white reveals the layer to which the mask is attached. Concealing more of the layer above reveals any layers that are below. This makes it possible to blend images together.

But layer masks aren't just black and white, they are grayscale, just like alpha channels. And this means that you can paint on a layer mask in shades of gray to *partially conceal* or *partially reveal* that layer.

Layer Mask Essentials

Let's take a look at layer mask conventions and terminology, beginning with a couple of housekeeping points:

- The Background layer—that layer that most Photoshop images start out with—doesn't support transparency and thus can't support layer masks. It sounds worse than it is: to add a layer mask to a Background layer, take the simple step of first converting that layer to a "normal" layer by double-clicking the layer thumbnail and renaming the layer. Alternatively, Option/Alt-double-click the layer thumbnail.

- The checkerboard pattern is how Photoshop represents transparency. While this is conceptually useful to distinguish transparent pixels from opaque white pixels, it can be visually distracting. To change the way transparency is represented, choose Photoshop > Preferences > Transparency & Gamut (Windows: Edit > Preferences > Transparency & Gamut) and change the grid size. Choose None if you don't want to see a checkerboard.

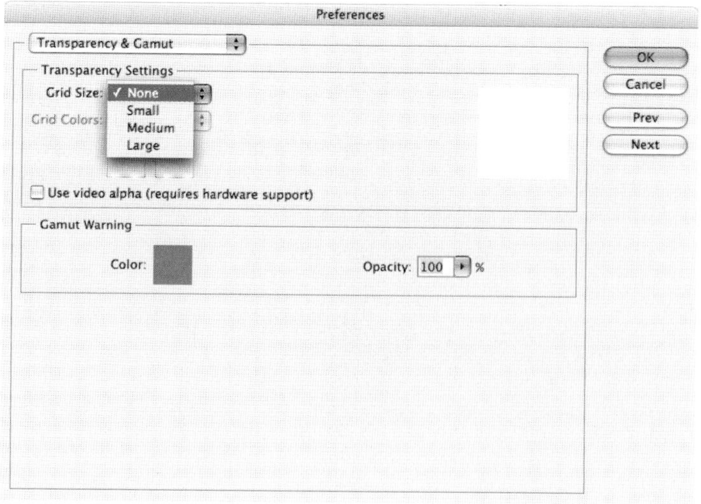

FIGURE 4.3 Transparency & Gamut Preferences. If you find the checkerboard distracting, choose None for your Transparency Settings.

Creating and Deleting Layer Masks

Now let's take a look at the basics of how to create layer masks:

- To turn an active selection into a layer mask, click the Add layer mask icon at the bottom of the Layers palette. This reveals the selection and masks everything that was not selected. If you have selected the inverse of your subject, hold Option/Alt as you click the Add layer mask icon. This conceals the selection and masks everything that was selected. I recommend that you always use the first approach, if necessary inversing your selection beforehand. Here's why: if you make a mask by hiding the selection (holding Option/Alt), the layer mask stops at the edges of the image. This is rarely a problem, but when it is, it can be quite perplexing. If you later move the layer, the edges of the layer mask become visible. Once the edges of the mask become visible, should you apply blurring to the layer mask, but these newly visible edges may show up as faint lines on your image.

A

Add layer mask icon

B

FIGURE 4.4 The dolphin was masked by selecting its background and then adding a layer mask while holding down Option/Alt to hide the selection (example **A**). Faint lines show because the layer mask has been blurred and moved—you can tell it's been moved by looking at the layer mask thumbnail (example **B**). Solution: Make your masks by revealing the selection, i.e., not holding down Option/Alt, if necessary inversing your selection first.

- Alternatively, you can add a layer mask using the menus. Select Layer > Layer Mask and choose the appropriate option from the submenu. That's if you like doing things the hard way. Reveal All gives you a mask where all the pixels are white, that is, nothing is yet masked. Hide All is the opposite—all pixels black, or everything masked. Reveal Selection yields a mask with the pixels of your active selection white and everything else black; Hide Selection is the opposite.

- To delete a layer mask, drag its thumbnail to the Trash icon at the bottom of the Layers palette. You see a warning dialog asking if you want to Delete or Apply the layer mask. Choose Delete and the layer mask is gone and the layer returned to its original state; choose Apply and the masked portions of the layer are deleted—use with extreme caution. If you hold down Option/Alt as you drag the layer mask thumbnail to the Layers palette's Trash, the layer mask is deleted without the warning dialog. Layer masks are removed (and applied) when you merge or flatten layers.

Viewing and Editing Layer Masks

Here are some techniques for nimbly viewing and editing your layer masks:

- As your images get more complex, with multiple layers and multiple layer masks, it's useful to change your viewing perspective and remind yourself exactly how your image is constructed. To disable or enable a layer mask, Shift-click the layer mask thumbnail in the Layers palette—a red X will show on the layer mask thumbnail.

- To view just layer mask, Option/Alt-click layer mask thumbnail in the Layers palette. Option-click the layer mask thumbnail again to return to the image.

- Like alpha channels, layer masks show up in the Channels palette (with their names italicized) when the layer is selected. To view them as a transparent overlay, just like a Quick Mask, click the visibility icon of the Layer Mask channel.

- Just as with Quick Masks or alpha channels, you can paint on a layer mask with any of your painting tools, or you can use the selection tools and then press Option/Alt-Delete to fill your resulting selection with the foreground color or Command/Ctrl-Delete to fill with the background color. You can also paint with your Gradient tool to get seamless transitions between images, most usefully with a Foreground to Transparent gradient. This gradient lets you build up the gradient in multiple swipes, making it easier to get the effect you're after (unlike a Foreground to Background gradient which, each time you use it, replaces what you did before).

- By default, layer masks are linked to their respective layers. This means that as you move, scale, or in any way transform a layer, its layer mask is correspondingly moved, scaled, or transformed. If you want to move the layer independently of the layer mask, uncheck the linking icon.

- To move a layer mask to another layer, drag the mask thumbnail to the other layer. To copy the layer mask to another layer, hold down Option/Alt as you drag the mask thumbnail to the other layer.

- To convert a layer mask to an active selection, which you can then use on any layer in your image, Command/Ctrl-click the Layer Mask thumbnail. Holding down Shift or Option/Alt at the same time adds or subtracts the selection from a currently active selection.

- Mask multiple layers by adding a layer mask to a layer group rather than a specific layer.

- Working with layer masks, it's easy to get confused about what you have selected—the layer or the layer mask—and consequently where you are adding paint. As well as the document title bar saying Layer (name), Layer Mask, Photoshop offers another visual cue that is a little on the subtle side, as you can see in the following figures.

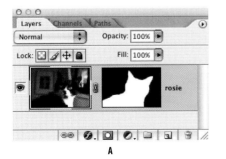

A

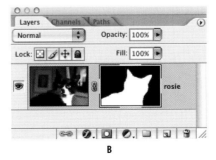

B

FIGURE 4.5 The layer is targeted: note the borders around the layer thumbnail (example **A**). The layer mask is targeted—borders around the layer mask thumbnail (example **B**).

Layer Mask Shortcuts

When working with layer masks you can change several variables: foreground color, brush size, brush hardness, and opacity. It's a good idea to get familiar with the shortcuts.

Toggle Foreground/Background Color: x

Change the Brush Size: left bracket [to go smaller, right bracket] to go bigger.

Painting with a brush hardness of less than 100% on the layer mask softens the mask edges with feathering effects. To change the Brush Hardness: Shift [to go softer in 25% increments, Shift] to go harder in 25% increments. Unless your subject that you are masking has some edges that should be sharp and others that should be softer, keep the brush hardness consistent. Typically I find a 75% hardness works well.

Restore Foreground/Background color to Default Black and White: d

Painting with a brush opacity of less than 100% on a layer mask is a great way to achieve transparency effects. The higher the brush opacity the more is revealed or concealed. To change brush opacity, use your keypad numbers: 1 = 10%, 5=50%, 0=100%, etc.

You can access the layer mask of a selected layer by pressing Command/Ctrl-\.

Creating a Simple Composite

Let's take a look at some of things we can do with layer masks, beginning with this simple composite of a cheery-looking viewer and a bright blue sky.

web files

1. Open the source images, the smiley face viewer and blue sky.

2. Using the Move tool (v) drag the smiley viewer on top of the clouds image. Hold Shift to register the two layers, i.e., so that one fits exactly on top of the other. Double-click the layer thumbnails to name the layers.

A   **B**   **C**

3. Make a selection of the viewer using the Magnetic Lasso tool. Alternatively, if you're comfortable with using the Pen tool, make a pen path around the viewer and convert this to a selection by choosing Make Selection from the Paths palette menu. For a discussion of drawing pen paths see the section "Drawing with the Pen Tool" in Chapter 1, "Selections." Feathering selections is also discussed in Chapter 1.

4. Apply a feather radius for a better transition between the selection edge and the background; I applied a feather radius of 1 pixel.

FIGURE 4.6 The source images (examples **A** and **B**) and the finished composition (example **C**).

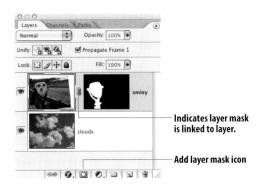

Indicates layer mask is linked to layer.

Add layer mask icon

FIGURE 4.7 The Layers palette showing the layer mask applied to the smiley layer.

5. Click the Add Layer Mask icon at the bottom of the Layers palette to reveal the selection and hide, or mask, the non-selected parts of the Smiley
layer. This reveals the Clouds layer below. For the opposite effect—hiding
the selection and revealing the non-selected areas—Option/Alt -click the
Add layer mask icon.

FIGURE 4.8 Viewing the layer
mask by itself: Option/Alt-click
to toggle between the layer
mask and the image.

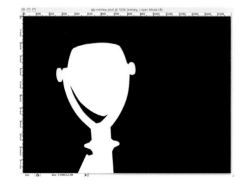

6. Optionally, to view just the layer mask, Option/Alt-click the layer mask
thumbnail. (Option/Alt-click again to return to the image). Viewing the
layer mask thumbnail helps when refining the mask and for understanding how the layer mask is working.

7. Make your finishing touches. I couldn't resist: I moved and rotated the
smiley. Because the layer mask is linked to the layer, the layer mask was
moved and rotated along with it (see Figure 4.7). I applied some color correction using a Curves adjustment layer, changed the color of the viewer
using a Hue/Saturation adjustment layer, and sharpened the Smiley layer
with the Unsharp Mask Filter (Filter > Sharpen > Unsharp Mask). Adjustment layers are discussed in detail in Chapter 5, "Adjustment Layers."

Combining Textures

In this next example we'll see how painting in shades of gray allows you to introduce transparency effects: Darker grays conceal more, lighter grays reveal more of the layer. Or put another way, the closer you move towards black, the greater the masking effect; the closer you move towards white, the more the revealing effect.

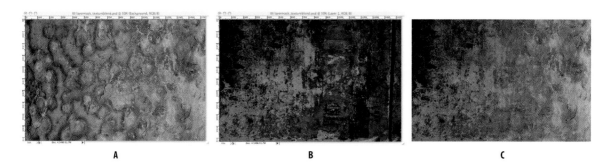

A   B   C

1. Open the source images, Texture 1 and Texture 2.

2. Using the Move tool (v) drag one image on top of the other. Hold down the Shift key to register the layers. Double-click the layer thumbnails to rename the layers.

3. Select the top layer and click the Add Layer Mask icon at the bottom of the Layers palette to add a layer mask to this layer.

4. Choose the Gradient tool (g), and from the Gradient Picker choose Foreground to Transparent (the second in the list), and for gradient type choose Linear. Make sure that the Transparency option is checked. Make Black the foreground color. Target the layer mask and swipe across the image with the Gradient tool. The farther you drag, the more gradual the transition; if you don't like the result, press Command/Ctrl-Z to undo and try again, or just swipe again with the Gradient tool for a cumulative effect. Where the gradient is black on the layer mask, that portion of the layer is concealed, revealing portions of the layer beneath.

FIGURE 4.9 The source images (examples **A** and **B**) and the finished composition (example **C**).

web files

5. As an optional step, once you've got the gradient more or less the way you like it, you can further tweak the way the gradient transitions from black to transparent—and consequently how the image layers blend together—using Levels or Curves on the layer mask itself. That's right: as well as painting on masks you can also make tonal adjustments on a mask. With the layer mask selected choose Image > Adjustments > Levels to see how moving the Input sliders affects the ratio of black to white in the mask and how that in turn impacts the image.

FIGURE 4.10 The Gradient tool options showing a Foreground to Transparent gradient and Linear Gradient. Transparency is checked.

FIGURE 4.11 The Layers palette of the image showing the layer mask with gradient and the mask itself. Option/Alt-click the layer mask to toggle between viewing the mask and the image.

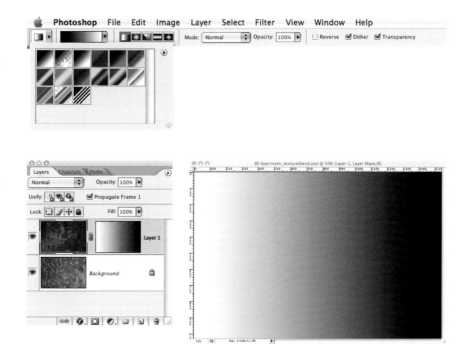

Layer masks can be a bit puzzling—especially late at night and on deadline. Don't sweat it: you have the History palette as a safety net and, more importantly, everything you do on a layer mask is undoable—if you mask too much of the image by painting on the layer mask in black, painting the layer mask in white reverses that.

Choking a Mask

In Chapter 1, "Selections," we saw how we can contract a selection to bring the selection edge slightly inside the subject shape. This prevents color fringing by excluding any background colors. A more visual and flexible way of achieving the same end is to choke a mask. I prefer to perform this step on a layer mask, but you can also choke a Quick Mask or an alpha channel. Here's a simple example:

FIGURE 4.12 The source image.

web files

1. Open the Metro image.

2. Make a selection of the Metro sign. Because of its graceful curves and straight lines, the Pen tool is a good choice, but the Magnetic Lasso also works. If you use the Pen tool, convert your Work Path to a selection by choosing Make Selection from the Paths palette. Choose a feather radius of 0—we'll be adding the feathering later.

3. Switch to Quick Mask to refine your selection as necessary.

4. When satisfied with the selection, switch back to Standard mode and convert the selection to a layer mask. Option/Alt-double-click the Background layer and then click the Add Layer Mask icon at the bottom of the Layers palette.

5. To evaluate the quality of your mask, it can help to see your subject against a contrasting color. Create a new layer. Choose a bright color from your Swatches palette and press Option/Alt-Delete to fill this layer with the color. Drag the layer beneath the Metro layer in the Layers palette.

FIGURE 4.13 Putting the subject on a temporary color layer highlights inaccuracies in the mask.

6. Select the layer mask and choose Filter > Blur > Gaussian Blur. I used an amount of 2 pixels.

7. With the layer mask selected, choose Image > Adjustments > Levels or Command/Ctrl-L and move the Black point slider and Mid point slider to the right. Watch the document window carefully and you should see the mask contracting around the Metro sign. The farther you drag the sliders the more the mask contracts. Note that moving the White point slider and Mid point slider to the left has the opposite effect, i.e., spreading or expanding the selection.

8. Discard the temporary color layer by dragging its thumbnail to the Trash icon at the bottom of the Layers palette.

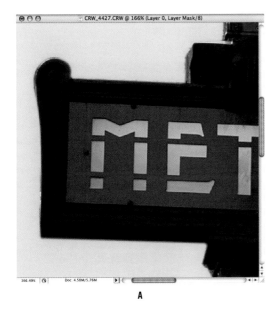

A

B

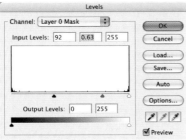

C

FIGURE 4.14 Choking the mask before (example **A**) and after moving the Levels Input sliders as indicated (examples **B** and **C**).

Looking Through (and Breaking Out of) the Top Layer

When trying to grasp the concept of layer masks, it can help to think of them as windows to the layers below. Let's look at a literal window.

A   B   C

FIGURE 4.15 The source images (examples **A** and **B**) and the finished composition (example **C**).

web files

1. Open the Window and Burger Man images.

2. Using the Move tool (v), drag the window image onto the Burger Man image, holding down the Shift key to align the two layers. Double-click the layer thumbnails to rename the layers.

3. Make a selection of the window shapes. I used the Magic Wand, Shift-clicking to pick up each successive pane, and Shift-clicking again to pick up any stray areas. Make sure Contiguous is checked, otherwise your selection will spill outside the window shapes.

FIGURE 4.16 The windows selected.

4. Inverse the selection; then click Add Layer Mask on the bottom of the Layers palette to convert your selection into a layer mask.

5. Soften the selection edges and help them blend more convincingly with the layer below by choking the mask as outlined in the previous section, Choking a Mask.

6. Now for the tricky bit: hide the window layer and make a selection of the burger man's arm. With this selection active, turn the visibility of the window layer back on and target the window layer mask. Make Black your foreground color and press Alt-Delete to fill the selection. The arm should now come through the window. You'll probably need to refine the window layer mask by painting in black to reveal more of the arm, or in white to reveal more of the window.

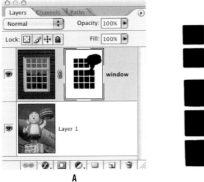

A   B

FIGURE 4.17 The Layers palette (example **A**) and the resulting layer mask (example **B**).

Blending Shape and Texture

A simple and effective use of layer masks is to blend two or more images together to create something greater than the sum of its parts.

In this example I'm mixing a Granny Smith and an orange to create a new hybrid fruit. This technique is applicable when combining any similarly shaped but distinctly different objects.

FIGURE 4.18 The source images (examples **A** and **B**) and the finished hybrid fruit (example **C**).

Using the Move tool (v) I dragged the orange image on top of the apple, holding Shift to align the two layers.

ISTOCKPHOTO.COM

A   B   C

With Free Transform (Edit > Free Transform or Command/Ctrl-T), I distorted the orange so that it was more or less the same shape as the apple and slightly overlapped the edges of the apple. It was helpful to temporarily reduce the opacity of the orange layer to see the apple beneath.

FIGURE 4.19 Transforming the orange to correspond with the size and shape of the apple.

To retain the shadow of the apple and to make the orange fit exactly into the apple shape, I made a selection of the apple (excluding the shadow) and then, instead of masking the apple itself, targeted the orange layer and added a layer mask to that layer. This is the punch line of this example: you can make a selection on one layer and apply it as a layer mask on another.

To make a transition between the two fruits, I used the Foreground to Transparent gradient on the layer mask of the orange layer. To constrain the gradient to the fruit shape, I turned the mask into an active selection by Command/Ctrl-clicking the layer mask thumbnail.

The gradient transition was a good start, but I found it was also necessary to shape the transition with a large soft-edged brush, painting around the stem area.

To complete the composite, the shadow needed to reflect orange as well as green: I used Quick Mask to make a selection of the shadow on the apple layer and then copied this to a new layer: Layer > New > Layer via Copy or Command/Ctrl-J. I locked the transparency of this layer, then sampled color from the orange with the Eyedropper tool (i), and painted over the shadow. Lastly, I turned the blend mode of the shadow layer to Color and reduced its opacity to about 20%.

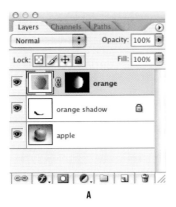

A

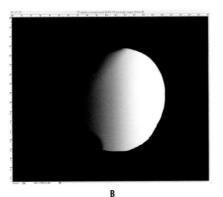

B

FIGURE 4.20 The Layers palette (example **A**) and the orange layer mask (example **B**).

Blending Different Exposures

Layer masks make it possible to combine different exposures of the same image. This is especially useful when you have an image that has deep shadows as well as bright highlights.

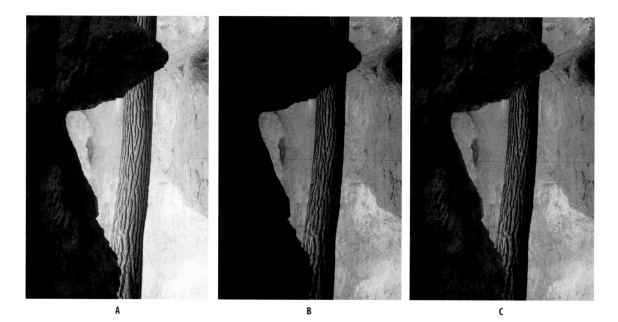

A   B   C

FIGURE 4.21 The source images (examples **A** and **B**) and the finished composition (example **C**).

This picture of Bryce Canyon contains a very dark foreground shape. The image was scanned from a transparency, and no matter how I tweaked the scanner software, I got one of two unacceptable results: if the scanner software was adjusted to capture the bright values of the background rock and the tree, the foreground shape became a dark blob that held no detail, or if the scanner software was adjusted to capture the foreground, the background became overexposed. The solutions: scan the image twice; or if working with a Camera RAW file, open two versions of the image—one that captures highlight detail, the other that captures shadow detail.

1. Open the source images, Bryce Bright and Bryce Dark.

2. Using the Move tool (v) drag the foreground (bright) image onto the background (dark) image, holding down the Shift key to align the layers.

3. On the top layer make a selection of the rock shape on the left—I used the Pen tool, then converted the path into a selection, but the Magnetic Lasso also works.

4. Click Add Layer Mask, at the bottom of the Layers palette, to convert the selection into a mask, revealing the rock and letting the tree and background rock from the layer beneath show through.

5. As a finishing touch to feather the transition between the two layers, apply a 1.5-pixel Gaussian Blur to the layer mask.

Replacing Parts of an Image

A particularly effective way to replace a portion of an image is using the Paste Into command, which creates a layer mask based on your active selection. A common usage of this feature is to replace a washed out or monochromatic sky with a more dramatic or colorful sky from another image.

web files

FIGURE 4.22 The Layers palette showing how the image is constructed.

A   B   C

FIGURE 4.23 The source images with washed out sky (example **A**) and the more dramatic sky that will replace it (example **B**). The finished composition (example **C**).

web files

1. Open the Beach Huts and Sky images.

2. In the beach huts image that contains the boring sky, make a selection of the sky. If you are working with an image where the sky is completely washed out, the Magic Wand tool may be adequate; otherwise, you might need the Pen tool (p) or a Quick Mask (q) for a more complex selection.

3. Open the sky image and select the portion of the sky you want and copy it to the clipboard, Edit > Copy (Command/Ctrl-C).

4. Return to the beach huts image and choose Edit > Paste Into. The sky image is added to a new layer with the inverse of the sky selection from the Beach Huts layer used to mask the new sky where it overlaps the background layer.

5. To reposition the new sky within the shape of the layer mask, click the layer thumbnail and drag using the Move tool (v) in the document window to move the sky around. When using Paste Into, the layer and layer mask of the new layer are not linked.

6. Check the edges where the new sky and buildings meet at a high view percentage. To avoid any fringing of the original background color, set the blend mode of the sky layer to Multiply (combining the new sky with the featureless old one) and as necessary paint around the edges of the layer mask with the Blur tool (r) to blend any areas where you can see the join.

FIGURE 4.24 Choose the Paste Into command to add the sky image to the new layer.

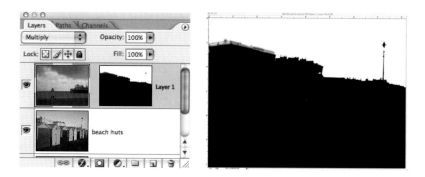

FIGURE 4.25 The image layers and the layer mask added by choosing Paste Into and then refined by using the Blur tool around parts of the edge to achieve a seamless blend between the new sky and the buildings of the original image.

In a similar vein, you might want to composite elements from two or more shots of the same subject in order to use the best parts of each. Take this family portrait, for example.

A B C

In example A the older child is looking away from the camera; in example B Mom is pulling a funny face. The simple solution is to make a selection of the boy's head (example B) and drag this to the other image. Include a generous amount of the background around the boy's head because this gives you more flexibility when blending the new head with the layer below.

FIGURE 4.26 We want to take the boy's head from example **B** and composite it with example **A**. The finished result, example **C**, is sharpened with the background slightly blurred.

FIGURE 4.27 The Layers palette showing how the image is constructed.

Blend the copied head with the background image. In Figure 4.28 I have circled the joins. Adding a layer mask and painting in black over these areas with a soft-edged black brush does the trick.

FIGURE 4.28 Mask out the joins by painting in black on a layer mask.

Creating Painterly Effects

There's an infinite number of effects you can achieve with layer masks. In this example I use a layer mask to blend a photograph and a line art version of that same image.

FIGURE 4.29 The original image (example **A**) and the finished effect combining line art and photograph (example **B**).

A

B

web files

1. Open the Daffodil image.

2. Duplicate the background layer and apply an Unsharp Mask filter to the copy. I used an Amount of 20, a Radius of 60, and a Threshold of 0. Rename this layer "Sharpened."

3. Duplicate the sharpened layer and choose Filter > Stylize > Find Edges to convert the layer to line art.

4. Because Find Edges introduces distracting colors into the composition, choose Image > Adjustments > Desaturate (Command/Ctrl-Shift-U) to desaturate the layer.

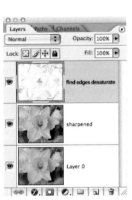

FIGURE 4.30 Find Edges applied to a duplicate layer and desaturated.

5. Here's the good bit: add a layer mask to the Find Edges layer and paint on that layer mask. Experiment with different brush types—I used a large charcoal brush available from the Brushes palette—to reveal the yellow daffodil beneath.

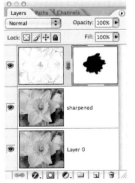

FIGURE 4.31 Painting on the layer mask of the Find Edges layers.

6. To restore the line art edges, make a copy of the Find Edges layer, delete its layer mask by dragging its thumbnail to the Trash icon at the bottom of the Layers palette (don't choose Apply), and change the layer blend mode to Multiply.

FIGURE 4.32 Duplicating the Find Edges layer and setting the blend mode to Multiply restores the line detail.

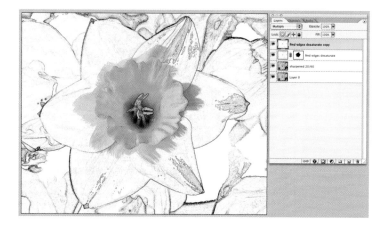

Selective Filtering

In the previous example we saw how we can use layer masks to paint in—or paint out—one version of an image over another version of the same image. We can use this method to paint in the effects of any filter, allowing us to apply our filters selectively and at any time change how much of the filtering effect we choose to reveal. Here are just three examples chosen from hundreds of possibilities. In each case the approach is the same. Feel free to use your own images here.

1. Duplicate the layer (Command/Ctrl-J).

2. Apply the filter to the duplicate layer.

3. Add a layer mask to the duplicate layer and paint in black to mask portions of the filter layer. Or, if you want less than 50% of the filter layer, fill its layer mask with black and then paint in white to reveal the effects of the filter.

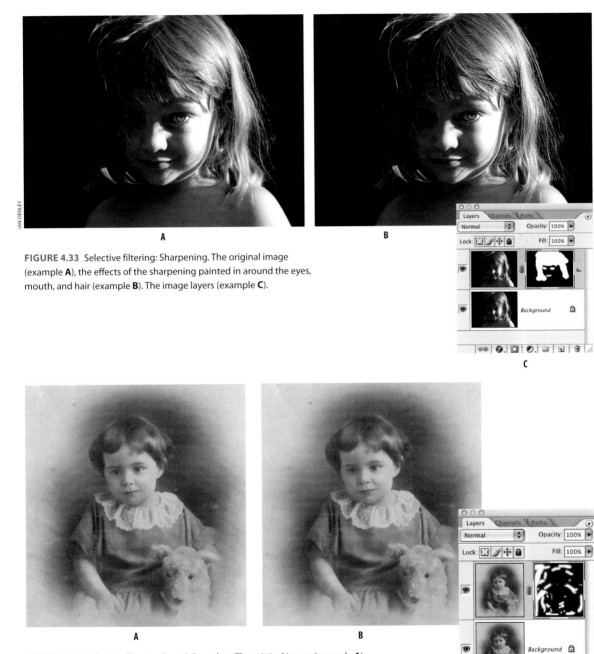

FIGURE 4.33 Selective filtering: Sharpening. The original image (example **A**), the effects of the sharpening painted in around the eyes, mouth, and hair (example **B**). The image layers (example **C**).

FIGURE 4.34 Selective filtering: Dust & Scratches. The original image (example **A**), the effects of the sharpening painted in the background areas where there is little detail. Major creases and defects in areas of detail would need to be addressed with the Patch tool and Healing Brush (example **B**). The image layers (example **C**).

A B C

FIGURE 4.35 Selective filtering: Graphic Pen. The original image (example **A**), the effects of the graphic pen painted out with a gradient on the layer mask revealing the image to the right (example **B**). Note, the graphic pen layer is set to Overlay blend mode and the opacity reduced to 50% in the image's layers (example **C**).

Adding Custom Borders

Border effects? Layer masks are the answer, and the reason is that you can apply filters to your layer masks just as you would to an image, the difference being that because you're working on a mask your filtering is nondestructive. Photoshop comes with a set of Frame Actions that automates this process, but creating your own frame and edge effects is a good way to appreciate how layer masks work.

FIGURE 4.36 I added a spattered edge to this photo of Brighton West Pier at sunset by applying a Spatter filter to the layer mask.

1. Open the Brighton image.

2. Select the whole canvas by pressing Command/Ctrl-A, then choose Select > Transform Selection to reduce this active selection to about 80% of the size of the canvas. Hold the Option/Alt key to scale the selection from the center of the image.

3. Convert the layer to a normal layer by Option/Alt-double-clicking the layer name. Click Add a mask to turn the selection into a layer mask hiding the nonselected area.

4. Select the layer mask and choose Filter > Filter Gallery to experiment with applying filters to the mask. The frame effect is created by roughing up the edge of the layer mask, spreading the white into the black, and vice versa. I chose Brush Strokes > Spatter filter. Alternatively, you can paint on the layer mask with a textured brush. At the bottom of the Brushes palette menu you have the option to load various styles of brushes.

web files

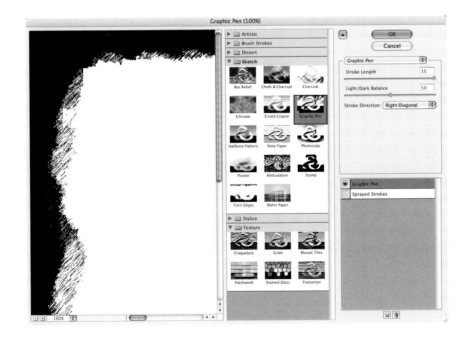

FIGURE 4.37 Experimenting with the Filter Gallery.

FIGURE 4.38 A brushed border created with a round bristle brush. I went around the edge once with 100% opacity and then again with 50% opacity.

FIGURE 4.38 A brushed border created with a round bristle brush. I went around the edge once with 100% opacity and then again with 50% opacity.

Creating Panoramas

Photoshop's feature called Photomerge allows you to easily create panoramas by stitching together a series of images into an (almost) seamless whole. A successful panorama requires a bit of planning. For best results use a tripod, preferably with a level, and shoot each frame vertically—neither of which I did in the following example. If that's not possible, you can still create panoramas, but you (and Photoshop) are going to have to work harder to get a good result. When shooting the individual frames make sure you have a generous overlap—25 to 30% works well.

FIGURE 4.39 The original pieces from which the panorama is assembled (examples **A** through **E**).

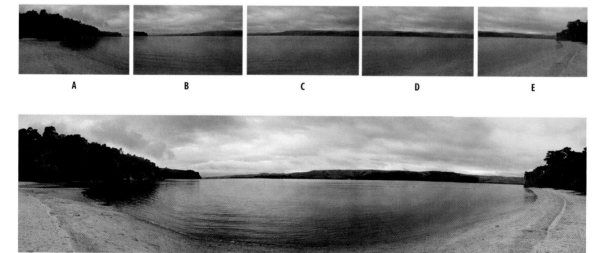

FIGURE 4.40 The completed panorama, sharpened and color corrected.

1. In this exercise, you'll use your own images. From within Adobe Bridge, select the thumbnails of the images you want to make up your panorama and choose Tools > Photoshop > Photomerge. (You can also use Photomerge directly from within Photoshop—File > Automate > Photomerge—but you have to either open all the images first or navigate to the images from within the Photomerge dialog.)

2. Photomerge gives its best shot at joining the images together. Any images it doesn't know what to do with appear at the top of the Photomerge dialog box.

3. If you're dissatisfied with Photomerge's attempts, position the individual images yourself. Using the Arrow tool drag the thumbnail(s) to the top of the Photomerge window, then turn off Snap to Image and drag them into position in the main window.

4. As necessary, use the Rotate Image tool to rotate pieces, although for fine-tuning you're better off using Free Transform in Photoshop. In this example, because I used automatic exposure on my camera, some segments are lighter than others; Photomerge's attempt at blending these different exposures results in the segments looking like triangles stitched together. Ideally I should have used manual exposure to begin with—taking the exposure readings from the first segment and using them for the subsequent segments; because I didn't, I'm going to have work harder to make my blends seamless.

FIGURE 4.41 The Photomerge dialog box: Be sure to check Keep as Layers so that you can easily edit the result.

5. Rather than settle for Photomerge's blending, which is never perfect, for better results, blend the images yourself using—you guessed it—layer masks. Be sure to check Keep as Layers. If you choose Advanced Blending, you cede control of the blending to Photomerge, which is a bit of a crapshoot; personally, I've never had good results with this option and unfortunately it can't be combined with the Keep as Layers option.

6. When you're satisfied with the result, click OK to leave Photomerge and return to Photoshop, where you now have a layered image.

7. Add a layer mask (revealing all) to all except the bottom layer.

   The next part is tricky. Note, I am working left to right (that's how the panorama was shot) and from the bottom up through the layers.

8. Make an intersecting selection of the layer overlap and then paint within this selection on the layer mask with a Foreground to Transparent gradient. Here's how it works: Command/Ctrl-click the layer thumbnail of the bottom layer to turn its opaque pixels into a selection, then Command/Ctrl-Shift-click the thumbnail of the layer above to make a selection where the two layers overlap. Target the layer mask of the upper layer. Make black the foreground color. Choose the Gradient tool (g) and with a Foreground to Transparent linear gradient drag from left to right within this selection. I got the best results by beginning my gradient just outside the selection border and swiping the full width of the selection.

9. Repeat the previous step for each remaining layer in turn.

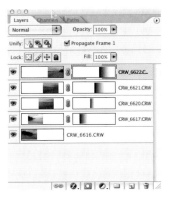

FIGURE 4.42 The Layers palette showing the layer masks, each with a Foreground to Transparent gradient applied.

10. Inspect the panorama closely to see what details do not marry up exactly from layer to layer. To fix these problems paint on the layer masks with a soft-edged brush. I also used the Healing Brush (j) on a separate layer to fix some problems with the sky.

FIGURE 4.43 Some doubling of the detail on the horizon can be seen. This can be fixed with a combination of painting with a brush on the layer masks and using the Healing Brush tool.

11. Complete any retouching. As finishing touches, I applied tonal and color correction as well as sharpening.

Isolating a Subject with a Cutout

When isolating a subject, remember this important adage: No one sees what you leave out. What's more, trying to include extraneous detail—or every single strand of hair—can sometimes result in an isolated subject that looks, well, a little odd. Taken out of their background—literally taken out of context—some subjects can look fake. For this reason, and also because edges are often contaminated with color spill from the original background color, it's often a good idea to make your selection edge slightly inside the subject.

Another important adage—and one that applies to every aspect of Photoshop, but particularly to making cutouts—is this: Know your intent. Knowing how you are going to use the resulting cutout determines how exacting you need to be when making it. For example, if you intend to place the cutout in a page layout against a solid and contrasting color, then you need to be more accurate than if the cutout will end up as part of a collage where any inaccuracies will likely be hidden by overlapping layers, or layer blend modes and opacity effects.

FIGURE 4.44 The original image (example **A**) and the finished cutout (example **B**).

A   B

web files

1. Open the Royal Pavilion image.

2. Because the subject is on a flat, homogenous background with good edge contrast, we can use the Magic Wand (w) and then choose Select > Inverse (Command/Ctrl-Shift-I) to select the subject.

3. Turn the Background layer to a normal layer by Option/Alt-double-clicking its thumbnail and click the Add Layer Mask icon to convert your active selection into a layer mask.

4. Apply a Gaussian Blur to the mask (1-2 pixels) to feather the mask edge. To choke the mask choose Levels (Command/Ctrl-L) and move the Black point and Mid point sliders to the right, keeping a careful eye on how this affects your selection edge. Click Add a mask to hide the image background—you should see the transparency checkerboard in its place.

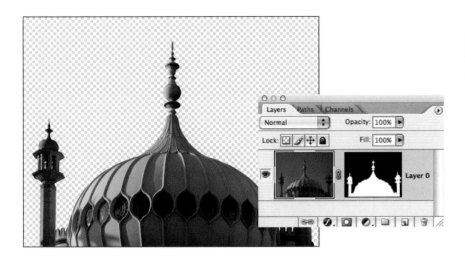

FIGURE 4.45 The resulting masked selection with the checkerboard representing the transparent pixels of the layer.

To place the image in InDesign or Quark (version 7 supports transparency) so that you can use it as part of a layout, save the image as a Photoshop (PSD) file or as a TIF with Save Transparency checked.

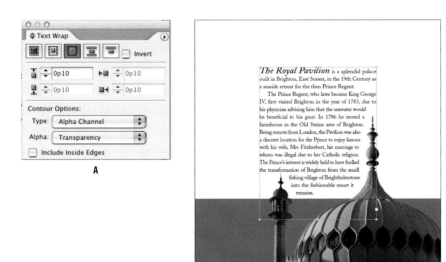

FIGURE 4.46 The Text Wrap palette (example **A**) and the image placed in InDesign (example **B**).

Using Transparency in InDesign

Importing a graphic with transparency into an InDesign layout allows you to use that transparency to create a text wrap around the graphic. Select the picture frame of your image and from the Text Wrap palette choose Wrap Around Object Shape. Then, to recognize the layer mask saved with the file, from the Contour Options pull-down menu choose Alpha Channel (aka your layer mask) and the text wraps around the image shape. Adjust the image offsets, or select the image with the Direct Selection tool and adjust the text wrap path to finesse the way your text rags around the image.

Combining Soft and Sharp Selection Edges

Sometimes one part of your selection edge is softer or sharper than the rest. Layer masks allow you to combine soft and sharp edges in the same selection. In this example, the top of the coffee cup is sharp focus while the base of the cup is in softer focus. To retain this quality in the layer mask we need to vary the softness of the mask edge.

FIGURE 4.47 The original image with the rim of the cup in sharper focus than the base (example **A**). The completed cutout image (example **B**).

A   B

web files

1. Open the Teacup image.

2. Make a pen path around the cup. Save the work path, then convert the save path to a selection with a feather radius of 0.

3. With the selection active, click the Add Layer Mask icon at the bottom of the Layers palette. Note: I have set my Transparency Grid settings to None because I find the checkerboard distracting.

4. Apply a 2-pixel Gaussian Blur to the layer mask to soften the whole selection edge slightly.

5. Open the Channels palette and click the Create new channel icon at the bottom of the palette. The new channel appears in solid black. Choose your Gradient tool (g) and, using a linear black to white gradient, drag from the top to the bottom of your canvas. This gradient alpha channel serves as the selection in the next step.

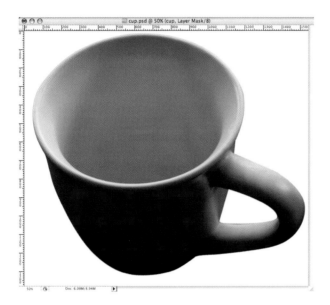

FIGURE 4.48 A layer mask added to the layer. No feathering is yet applied, hence the somewhat jagged edges.

6. Return to the layer mask and load the gradient alpha channel either by choosing Select > Load Selection or by Command/Ctrl-clicking its thumbnail in the Channels palette. With the selection active, hold down the Option/Alt key and choose Gaussian Blur from the top of the filter menu (at the top because it was the last filter used). Apply a value of about 8 pixels—your active selection graduates the effect of the filter so that the blurring is strongest at the bottom of the image. As an alternative, if you want to manually soften specific parts of a mask you can paint on the mask using the Blur tool.

The additional blurring has softened the mask towards the bottom of the cup, but it has also spread the selection, introducing some background colors.

7. To counteract the spread and introduction of background colors, choke the mask by using Levels on the layer mask and moving the Black and Mid point sliders to the right.

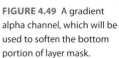

FIGURE 4.49 A gradient alpha channel, which will be used to soften the bottom portion of layer mask.

Making a "Pop-Out"

A pop-out is a commonly used technique in magazine and newspaper publishing where certain details of the image—a head, an arm, a leg—break out of the image's bounding rectangle. There are several ways (aren't there always?) to accomplish this. But if the image will be placed in a page layout program, the technique that offers the most design flexibility is to sandwich two versions of the image together in InDesign: one version is uncropped, the other has a layer mask defining which parts of the image are masked and which parts protrude outside of the bounding rectangle.

FIGURE 4.50 Two versions of the same streetcar: full frame (example **A**) and the other masked front (example **B**).

A   B

web files

1. Open the Streetcar image.

2. Duplicate the image (Image > Duplicate) and name this version Streetcar Masked.

3. Draw a pen path around the front of the streetcar. As insurance, double-click the work path to save it, then convert the path to a selection: from the Paths palette choose Make Selection and set the Feather radius to 0.

4. Click Add Layer Mask to convert the selection to a mask. Blur the mask with a Gaussian Blur of 1.5 pixels, then use Levels on the layer mask to choke the mask as necessary.

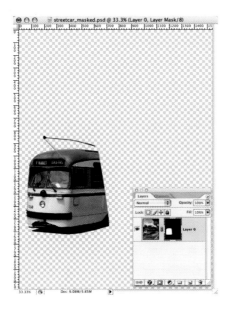

FIGURE 4.51 The front of the streetcar "cut out" with a layer mask.

5. Use the Blur tool (r) on the Layer Mask to soften the edge of the shadow at the front of the streetcar.

6. In InDesign, choose File > Place (Command/Ctrl-D) and position the uncropped version. Choose Edit > Copy (Command/Ctrl-C) and then Paste in Place (Command-Shift-Option-V/Ctrl-Shift-Alt-V) to paste a copy exactly on top of the original.

7. With the copy of the streetcar selected, choose Place again and, making sure you have Replace Selected Item checked, choose the cropped version of the streetcar. Nothing looks any different, but you now have the two versions of the streetcar, one on top of the other.

8. From the Object menu, choose Arrange > Send to Back to send the cropped version behind the uncropped version. Click away from your selection, then reselect the top (uncropped) version. Now you can adjust the size of the picture frame from the left, cropping the full-frame version and revealing the cropped portion beneath.

FIGURE 4.52 The finished pop-out in Adobe InDesign.

The historic streetcars of the F-line and the E-line serve San Francisco's main artery, Market Street, and its grand waterfront boulevard, The Embarcadero—linking San Francisco's most popular visitor attraction, Fisherman's Wharf, with its commercial, financial, and retail centers, and several residential neighborhoods along the route.

Vector Masking Sharp Edges and Curves

When you want to mask an object made up of sharply defined straight edges, graceful curves, or both, you create a sharp vector outline using a vector mask. Vector masks are essentially the same as layer masks with one crucial difference: the mask is made with vectors instead of pixels.

FIGURE 4.53 The guitar and a brown texture (examples **A** and **B**), soon to be combined.

A

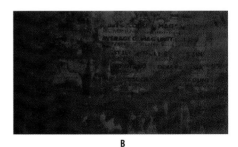

B

1. Open the Guitar and Brown Texture images.

2. Make a pen path selection around the guitar, then click Add Layer Mask twice—the first time gives you an empty layer mask, the second click converts your path to a vector mask. Alternately, choose Layer > Vector Mask > Reveal All.

web files

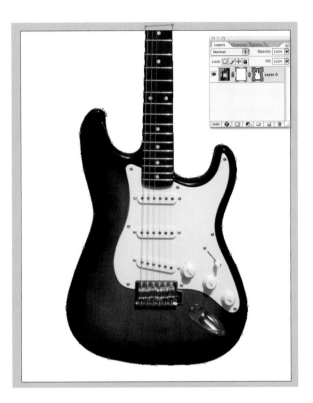

FIGURE 4.54 The guitar with vector mask.

Vector masks have hard, crisp edges—because they do not support transparency, you cannot feather their edges. Where vector masks have the edge (get it?) on layer masks is the degree of flexibility they offer when adjusting the mask: as you precisely adjust the pen path shape you can see instantly how this affects the image. For this reason, if you are comfortable working with the Pen tool, you might consider using vector masks as a stepping stone to a good layer mask. While there may be no substitute for the feathered edge of a layer mask, making the initial selection as a vector mask and then converting it to a layer mask is an efficient way of getting there.

3. To make any potential problems more visible, create a new layer beneath your subject layer and fill it with a bright color. Once you've tweaked the mask you can throw this layer away.

FIGURE 4.55 Fine-tuning the vector mask.

FIGURE 4.55 Fine-tuning the vector mask.

4. To convert a vector mask to a layer mask, choose Layer > Rasterize > Vector Mask.

5. When you are satisfied with the mask, drag the layer thumbnail of the guitar onto the texture image, and scale and rotate as necessary.

FIGURE 4.56 The finished composition, the guitar cutout with a vector mask.

Masking with Transparency

You can use the opaque pixels of one layer to mask other layers using a clipping mask (not to be confused with a clipping path, which is something different). The layer that is "clipping" other layers must have transparent areas and must be below the other layers. Put a layer (or layers) above this transparent layer and choose Layer > Create Clipping Mask (Command/Ctrl-Option/Alt-G) or Option/Alt-click the horizontal line between the two layers to clip the upper layer.

When a layer is clipped by another, the clipped layer (above) takes on the mask of the clipping layer (below).

Clipping masks are useful in the following situations:

- If you are using adjustment layers to make color adjustments and want to confine the adjustment to a specific layer rather than having it affect all layers below it. (More on this in the next chapter.)

- As an alternative to rasterizing Type or Smart Object layers, add a layer of color or texture above and have the Type or Smart Object layers clip those layers. If you edit your type, the changes are reflected on the clipping mask layer.

A

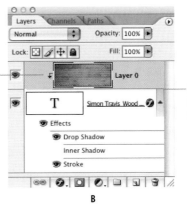

Put the layer you want to be "clipped" above the layer you want it to be "clipped by."

Option/Alt click the line between the layers to make a clipping mask.

FIGURE 4.57 I don't have to rasterize a Type layer to fill it with a texture (example **A**). Put the texture above the Type layer and make a clipping mask (example **B**).

B

■ If you have several layers that you want to clip to a particular shape.

FIGURE 4.58 To make this collage conform to the map shape (example **A**), I placed a vector drawing of the map on the bottom layer and made it clip the layers above. Example **B** shows the layers indented, clipped by the bottom layer.

A

B

FIGURE 4.60 On the Layers palette the thumbnails of layers that are grouped with or clipped by the layer beneath are shown indented.

Let's take a look at a scenario that uses both layer masks and clipping masks. In this reworking of Robert Indiana's famous LOVE graphic from the 1960s, I want each letter to take on a different texture. Where the texture is confined to the letter shape—as with the L and the E—this is easily achieved with a clipping mask: putting the texture layer above the letter layer and Option/Alt-clicking the line between the layers.

A

B

C

D

E

PHOTOS: ISTOCKPHOTO.COM

FIGURE 4.59 The four separate images used as background textures inside the letter shapes (examples **A** through **D**) and the finished composition (example **E**).

However, where I want the image to break out of the letter shape—as with the O and V—my best option is to use a layer mask. This is easy: Command/Ctrl-click the thumbnail for the Type layer to load it as an active selection. Target the image layer and click Add Layer Mask to mask that layer with the type shape. For the "breakout" on the O, I painted in white on the layer mask to restore one of the leaf shapes.

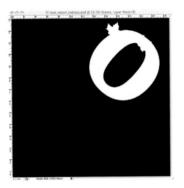

FIGURE 4.61 The O layer mask.

Where the tree breaks out of the V, it is necessary to load a pre-saved selection of the tree with its background knocked out. This is best done using a channel mask (see Masking Complex Detail in Chapter 6, "Channel Masking") made from a duplicate of the channels that offers the most edge contrast—in this case the blue channel.

Target the layer mask of the tree layer and load your saved selection: Command/Ctrl-click the alpha channel thumbnail or choose Select > Load Selection. Fill the active layer with white. To reduce the opacity of just the tree, Command/Ctrl-click the V to load the letter shape as a selection. Inverse this selection and then, on the V layer mask, paint in 30% black over the tree.

FIGURE 4.62 The V layer mask.

In Summary

Layer masks are the best (and safest) way to conceal specific parts of an image. Let the mantra, "Mask it, don't delete it," guide your Photoshop journey from now on. It's easy to make a selection into a layer mask (and vice versa). Working with the transparency implicit in layer masks gives you a world of possibility for blending images and compositing images, as I hope this small sampling of examples has shown. Mess around with them; use them to cut things out, to blend two or more images in ways that are both obvious and incongruous; use them to composite images in ways that may be goofy or classy. But whatever you do, make it seamless. And no matter what you do with layer masks, you'll be able to sleep more soundly knowing that you're applying your changes to the mask and not to the layer itself. Everything you do is undoable. As we'll see in the next chapter, when you combine layer masks with adjustment layers, a good thing gets even better. Oh, and just in case I didn't mention it enough times in this chapter: white reveals, black conceals.

CHAPTER 5

Adjustment Layers

THIS CHAPTER LOOKS AT USING ADJUSTMENT LAYERS to apply the big guns of tonal and color correction, Curves and Hue/Saturation, to "select" parts of an image by sampling brightness values or colors. While Curves, Hue/Saturation, and other adjustment options are not selection tools per se, they let you target specific tones and colors; often they are more effective (and much faster) than actually making area selections. For example, to increase the contrast in an area of sky, you may need only to apply a Curves adjustment that targets the specific tones of the sky. To change the colors of the subject of an image, perhaps you don't need to select it first, but can instead sample the colors and make a Hue/Saturation adjustment.

Rather than use the options under the Image > Adjustments menu, which permanently change the pixels in your photo, it's preferable to use adjustment layers to apply changes on the layer above your image. With adjustment layers you get to make the omelet without breaking the eggs—adjustment layers changes aren't permanently applied until flattening the image's layers, and you can change your mind as often as you like without damaging your pixels.

Effectively, this means unlimited undos. Compare this with Photoshop's other multiple-undos option, the History palette: you are limited to the number of history states you've set in the History palette, and, more importantly, they are only available until you've closed a document. An adjustment layer lets you change the adjustment at any time—weeks, months, or even years later. And because they leave your original image unharmed, adjustment layers make your workflow transparent: you can see exactly what's been done, especially if you name your adjustment layers to reflect what they do: for example, reduce blue, open shadows, lighten midtones, and so on.

There's more: In addition to letting you apply changes in a nondestructive way, each adjustment layer comes with a layer mask, which you can use (or not) to specify what parts of the layer are affected. Take the benefits of layers and combine them with the creative options of layer masks and you have some idea of what adjustment layers offer.

Adjustment Layers: Reasons to Be Cheerful

With adjustment layers the glass is always half full. You'd be crazy not to use them. Especially when you consider that they add almost no weight to the file size. Each adjustment layer is a simple instruction to move a slider, adjust a curve, or change a histogram. Because the adjustments are stored on their own layers, you have total flexibility. You can:

- Double-click the layer thumbnail at any time to revisit the adjustment and see exactly what settings you used.

- Use multiple adjustment layers to get the effect you're after.

- Turn off the adjustment layer to preview the image without the changes.

- Reduce the opacity of an adjustment layer to lessen its effect.

- Change the blend mode of an adjustment layer for a different effect. For example, applying a Curves adjustment for tonal correction sometimes also produces a slight, unwanted color shift. Change the blend mode of the adjustment layer to Luminosity and the color is unaffected; see Figure 5.1.

- Paint the layer mask that comes with the adjustment layer to control what parts of the underlying layer or layers are affected by the changes.

- Create a clipping mask from the adjustment layer to limit its influence to a single layer. Hold down Option/Alt as you choose the adjustment layer from the pop-up menu at the bottom of the Layers palette and check Use Previous Layer to Create Clipping Mask.

- Drag adjustment layers from one image to another.

A   B

FIGURE 5.1 The original image of these kids is very underexposed (example **A**). A drastically reshaped curve brings out detail (example **B**).

...and a Couple of Caveats

Surely there must be some cons to using adjustment layers. Actually, there are a couple:

- Adjustment layers do not travel across color-mode conversions. For example, changing from RGB to CMYK requires you either to discard your adjustment layers or burn them onto a flattened version of the file. In such situations, it's a good idea to save an RGB copy of the file before converting to CMYK; that way you retain your adjustment layers and have the option of returning to your file should you need to.

- Some features, such as Shadow/Highlight, aren't available as adjustment layers. Of course, you can duplicate the Background layer (Command/Ctrl-J), and then apply your Shadow/Highlight adjustment to the copied layer. Although you can't double-click to edit the adjustment, you can lower the opacity of the duplicated layer to lessen the effect, or change its blend mode for a different result.

Things to Know About Adjustment Layers

Here's some helpful information about adjustment layers:

- Adjustment layers affect all layers below but do not affect any layers above.

- Bitmap, Indexed Color, and Multichannel modes do not support adjustment layers.

- All files types that support layers allow you to save adjustment layers: Photoshop, TIF, EPS. JPEG does not, so if you are preparing a Web image using adjustment layers, save a copy in another file format.

- All of the following can be applied as adjustment layers: Solid Color, Gradient, Pattern, Levels, Curves, Color Balance, Brightness/Contrast, Hue/Saturation, Selective Color, Channel Mixer, Gradient Map, Photo Filter, Invert, Threshold, Posterize. The different types of adjustment layers overlap somewhat. For example, Brightness/Contrast, Levels, and Curves are all used for tonal correction; they come with ascending capability and complexity. I'm going to concentrate on Curves and Hue/Saturation as my preferred methods of adjusting tone and color in an image. For the most part, I find these two powerhouses give me all the options I need.

Using Curves to "Select" Tone and Color

Curves allow you to "select" specific tonal ranges in an image and modify them without affecting—or without affecting as much—the other tonal areas. For example, you can brighten the highlights without affecting the shadows and vice versa. In comparison, Brightness/Contrast either brightens or adds contrast to all the pixels in your image.

A   B   C

FIGURE 5.2 Luminosity Blend Mode. The original image (example **A**). A Curves adjustment applied to brighten the image also causes the train to take on a blue cast (example **B**). Changing the blend mode of the adjustment layer to Luminosity means that only the tone, not the color, is affected (example **C**).

Curves Explained

Here's a crash course in the Curves dialog box, shown in Figure 5.3 on the next page.

RGB images are measured in levels on a scale of 0-255. The gradient at the bottom of the Curves dialog box indicates which side is white (level 255) and which is black (level 0). You can switch the orientation of black and white by clicking the left triangle on the gradient. Doing so measures your image in ink percentages rather than brightness levels, applicable when editing CMYK images. All screenshots show RGB curves where white is on the right.

Curves begin as a 45-degree line indicating that no changes have been made (the output values equal the input values). An "S" curve adds contrast by brightening the highlights and deepening the shadows. See Figure 5.4.

As well as adjusting the composite RGB curve, you can work on each of the color channels independently by selecting a channel from the Channel pop-up menu at the top of the dialog box.

Levels does the same thing as Curves—selects specific tonal ranges in an image—but without the same degree of control. With Levels you work with a histogram that displays the number of pixels for each tonal value in the image. To see a histogram while using Curves, open the Histogram palette.

Work on the composite RGB Channel to
affect the tone or on the individual color
channels to color correct an image.

FIGURE 5.3 The Curves dialog box.

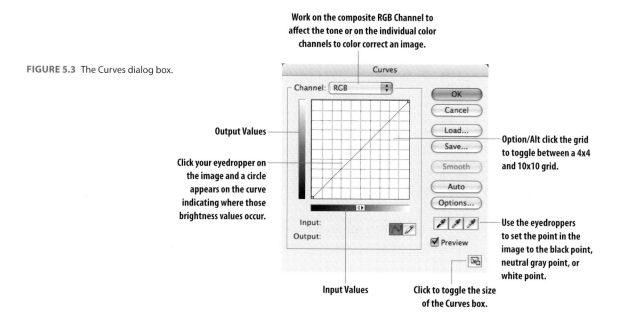

Output Values

Click your eyedropper on
the image and a circle
appears on the curve
indicating where those
brightness values occur.

Option/Alt click the grid
to toggle between a 4x4
and 10x10 grid.

Use the eyedroppers
to set the point in the
image to the black point,
neutral gray point, or
white point.

Input Values

Click to toggle the size
of the Curves box.

A

B

FIGURE 5.4 Applying an "S" curve. The original image
(example **A**). The S curve applied to boost brightness
and contrast (example **B**). And the Curve itself
(example **C**).

C

Use These Shortcuts in the Curves Dialog Box:

- Click a point on the curve and drag it up to brighten the image, drag down to darken the image. The brightening or darkening changes the image at the value specified. The effect on neighboring brightness values diminishes the farther those values are from the specified point.

- To target a specific tone while the Curves dialog box is open, Command/Ctrl-click the image to add a point on the curve precisely at that tone.

- To remove a point from the curve, simply drag it outside the grid.

- Option/Alt click the grid to toggle between a 4x4 or a 10x10 square grid.

Balancing Exposure

If you're like me you've probably got a shoebox (or its metaphorical equivalent) full of photographs where the foreground is underexposed due to your camera taking its light reading from the sky. This is the kind of problem an adjustment layer eats for breakfast. Let's take a look.

By putting down multiple anchor points on the curve you can edit the different tonal zones of your image with great independence. For example, using Curves you can edit the highlights without necessarily affecting the midtones or the shadows, or you can edit just the shadows without affecting the midtones or the highlights. The limitation of a Curves-only approach, however, is that anything more than a subtle change to either the shadows or highlights will also affect the tonal values at the other end of the tonal range, albeit to a lesser extent. With lots of practice you can carefully tweak the shape of your curve, adding up to 16 points (and Photoshop veterans perform amazing feats of independent tonal adjustment by carefully tweaking an image's curve!), but this is always time-consuming and not always successful. Curves that have been pulled up or down a lot at one end and locked down at the other tend to flatten the image in unpleasing ways. The good news is that you don't have to perform Curve gymnastics; instead, you can use the adjustment layer's mask to achieve the best result with the least effort.

For images with a clear division between highlight and midtones/shadows—pretty much any image with a sky or where the subject is strongly lit from one side—this is easy: just paint with a gradient on the layer mask. For images where the light and dark areas are mixed up, or where the subject extends above the horizon line into the sky, a gradient made from multiple swipes may work, or you may need to use your selection tools to make the mask. With the layer mask that comes free of charge with all adjustment layers, you can paint in black to block the effect of the adjustment layer wherever you don't want it to be applied to the image. Using adjustment layer masks to affect specific areas of an image combines the numerical approach of Curves with the select-by-area approach of layer masks.

In this example the sky is dramatic but the foreground dark. I underexposed this image intentionally. Had I exposed the image for the foreground, the sky would be too light, possibly blowing out the highlights, which would narrow my options for how I could edit the image. Underexposing the foreground is less problematic because it's easier to tease information from an underexposed than from an overexposed image. Assuming, that is, you're shooting the image with a half-decent camera. By the time I've performed a quick fix in Photoshop, I'll have the best of both worlds: a dramatic sky and a correctly exposed foreground.

web files

1. Open the Green Gulch image.

A   B

FIGURE 5.5 The original image with the underexposed foreground (example **A**). The foreground brightened using a Curves adjustment layer (example **B**); an adjustment layer mask restricts the influence of the adjustment layer.

2. Add a Curves adjustment layer. Move your pointer over the image to sample the tonal values from the dark areas of the foreground. Command/Ctrl-click to lock an anchor point on the curve at that particular brightness level. Pull up from the point to lighten the image. For now don't worry about what is happening to the sky; when you are happy with the way the foreground looks, click OK.

3. Choose your Gradient tool and a Foreground to Transparent gradient. Make sure that your foreground color is black. On the layer mask that came with the adjustment layer, drag down from the top to the bottom of the image. Wherever the gradient is black, the layer below will be protected from the effect of the Curves adjustment layer. You may need to have a few goes with the Gradient tool to get the black/transparent balance just right. Note that with a Foreground to Transparent gradient the swipes are cumulative, that is, each successive swipe adds to the existing gradient. If you use a Foreground to Background gradient, each swipe replaces the previous one.

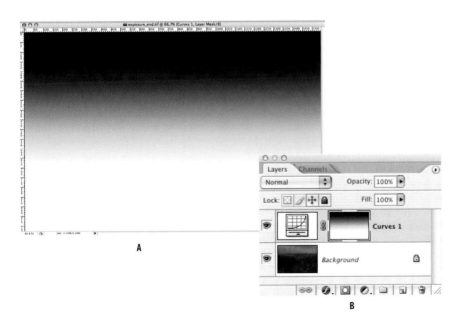

A

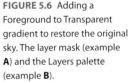

B

FIGURE 5.6 Adding a Foreground to Transparent gradient to restore the original sky. The layer mask (example **A**) and the Layers palette (example **B**).

Here's another example with a correctly exposed sky but underexposed foreground:

A   B

FIGURE 5.7 The original image (example **A**). The finished image (example **B**), which was easily fixed with a brightening curve and a Foreground (black) to Transparent gradient on a layer mask (examples **C** and **D**).

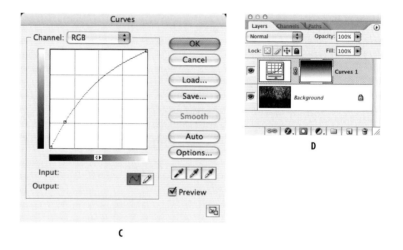

C   D

For more demanding images you can use a combination of layer masks and gradient layer masks to adjust the exposure in specific regions of the image. In the next example I brightened the foreground using a mask made from the sky. To brighten the doorway, I added another Curves adjustment layer. I filled the mask with black, and then, to reveal the brighten color in the doorway, I made several swipes with a White to Transparent gradient on the layer mask. Because the gradient transitions smoothly between white and black, no edges or halos appear around the mask.

A

B

C

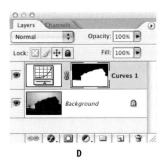

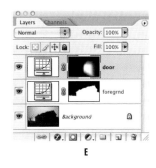

D

E

FIGURE 5.8 The original image (example **A**) and the finished image with brightened foreground and doorway (example **B**). One adjustment layer was used to brighten the foreground and another to brighten the doorway (examples **C**, **D** and **E**).

Removing a Color Cast

So far we've worked only on the composite RGB channel, but you will remember from Chapter 2, "Channels," that you can also work on specific color channels. This ability to target specific zones of specific channels is the foundation for color correction—if you have a red color cast, you pull down the curve of the Red channel.

Before we send out a posse to round up all our images with color casts, it's worth reflecting that not all color casts are bad. An orange color cast in a dramatic sunset picture, a yellow cast from late afternoon "magic light," a red cast from a concert photo taken under stage lights—they're all good. Bad color casts are the green complexions of people photographed under foliage, the jaundiced look of shots taken indoors under electric light, or the blue-rinse look your photos may have if the white balance of your camera was incorrectly set.

There are two basic approaches to removing a color cast: by the numbers and subjectively.

Color Correction by the Numbers

When color correcting by the numbers, you identify an area of your image—preferably a midtone area—that *should be* neutral gray. Neutral areas are made up of equal parts red, green, and blue. It doesn't matter exactly what the numbers are, just that they are the same. Adjusting individual color curves makes it possible to equalize the RGB levels at any point on your image, thus neutralizing these areas. Making such a change in the midtone area is usually enough to fix the color cast throughout the image, but if necessary you can also adjust highlights and shadows by shaping your curve accordingly.

The easiest types of images to correct by the numbers are those that include reference colors—areas we can confidently say should be neutral. Concrete or tarmac, for example, should be gray, and gray is neutral. Using your Color Sampler tool you can sample such an area. Then, using a Curves adjustment layer and your sample point and Info palette as references, you can make the RGB numbers equal to neutralize the color cast. Let's look at an example.

A   B

FIGURE 5.9 The original image has a strong blue cast (example **A**. In the color corrected version the Red, Green, and Blue values are equalized in the midtones (example **B**).

1. Open the Wine Cask image.

2. Using the Color Sampler tool, click the foreground—the concrete floor in front of the barrel. This will sample the color values at this point and display those values in your Info palette. To get the most accurate sample, set the options for the eyedropper to 3x3 Average.

3. Click the New Adjustment Layer icon at the bottom of the Layers palette and choose Curves. My sample shows that the Red and Green are similar in value, with the Green slightly higher. The Blue is much higher than both the Red and the Green. I want to bring the Red up to the Green, the median value, and the Blue down to the Green.

web files

4. While viewing the RGB curve, lock a point on each of the color curves by holding down Command/Ctrl-Option/Alt and clicking again on your sample point. Locking a point takes the guesswork out of finding exactly where the sample point occurs on each of the color curves. Because changing the Blue curve will have the most dramatic effect, let's do that one first.

5. To neutralize the Blue channel, choose Blue from the pop-up menu at the top of the Curves dialog box. Click the point on the curve; the Input and Output values are currently the same. The Input value should correspond to the Blue value of the sample point on your Info palette. If it doesn't—and it's possible you may be a digit or two off depending upon exactly where you clicked in the image—change the input value to match. Make the output value of the Blue curve the same as the input value of the Green curve. This change should go most of the way towards fixing the color cast.

FIGURE 5.10 Reducing the Blue curve (example **A**) and the Red curve (example **B**).

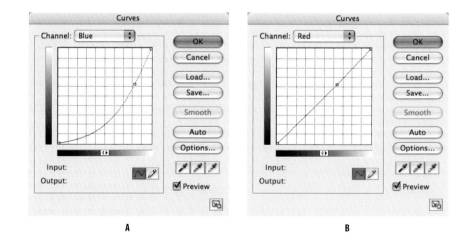

A   B

6. Repeat step 5 for the Red curve, changing its Output value at the sampled point to the Input value of Green. The Output values for your Red, Green, and Blue should now be the same (or within 1 or 2 levels of each other).

Subjective Color Correction

Sometimes a by-the-numbers approach doesn't cut it, and you'll want to tweak the color curves subjectively for a result that matches your expectations of the image. For example, in this desert shot, I know I want the sand to be more yellow. To add yellow I reduce its color complement, blue, by pulling down the Blue curve.

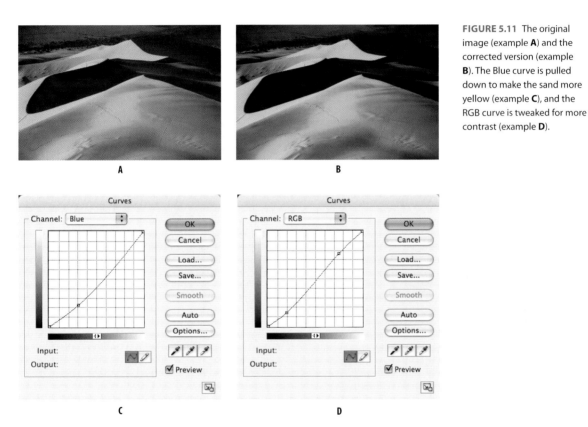

A   B

C   D

FIGURE 5.11 The original image (example **A**) and the corrected version (example **B**). The Blue curve is pulled down to make the sand more yellow (example **C**), and the RGB curve is tweaked for more contrast (example **D**).

Color correction is a complex and fascinating topic that I don't have the space (or the experience) to get into in any detail. But here's a useful quick guide. To remove a color cast, either reduce that color curve or add its complement

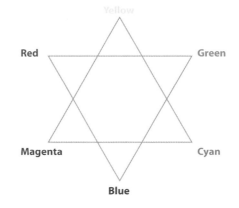

FIGURE 5.12 Color complements are at opposite points of this six-pointed star.

For example, if you're working on an RGB image that has too much red, simply pull down the Red curve. If the same image were in the CMYK color mode, which has no Red curve, instead increase the Cyan curve. If an RGB image has a yellow cast, pull up the Blue curve to add blue, so reducing the yellow; if the same image were in CMYK, simply pull down the Yellow curve.

Applying Curves to Adjustment Layer Masks

So if we should always apply tonal correction using adjustment layers, are the Curves and Levels options under the Image > Adjustments menu redundant? While you may never need them for tonal or color corrections to an image itself, they are still useful when adjusting the gray values of a layer mask or channel mask (see "Choking a Mask" in Chapter 4, "Layer Masks," and "Forcing Contrast" in Chapter 6, "Channel Masking")—since you can't apply adjustment layers to either layer masks or channel masks.

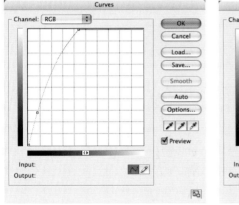

A

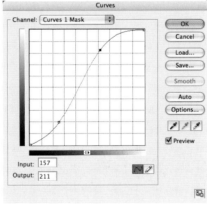

B

FIGURE 5.13 The original image (example **A**). A Curves adjustment layer is applied to lighten the foreground; a gradient layer mask restricts the effect of the adjustment layer to the bottom half of the image (examples **B** and **C**). Using Curves on the layer mask affects the transition from black (concealed) to white (revealed) (example **D**).

C

D

Selecting and Shifting Color with Hue/Saturation

To change the color of the subject of your image, your first instinct might be to select the subject—which, depending on its complexity, could be time-consuming. It could also be unnecessary. Sometimes the selection you're after is implicit in the image itself and you can use Hue/Saturation to adjust specific color in an image without so much as a trace of a marching ant.

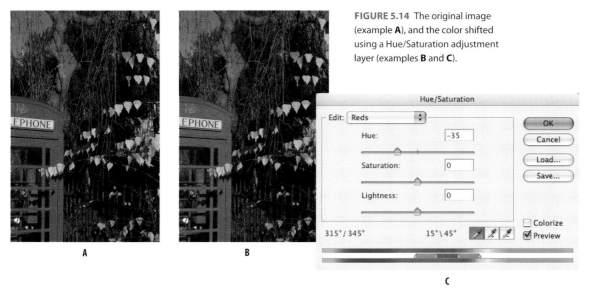

FIGURE 5.14 The original image (example **A**), and the color shifted using a Hue/Saturation adjustment layer (examples **B** and **C**).

A   B

C

web files

1. Open the Phone Box image. To change the color of the phone box it isn't necessary to first select it.

2. Add a Hue/Saturation adjustment layer and choose Reds from the Edit pop-up menu. Because the reds of the phone box are the only reds in the image, shifting the Reds will affect only the phone box. But before we do that, "Reds" is a very subjective term—we need to be more precise. Take your Hue/Saturation eyedropper and click an area of the phone box. The sliders on the color bar at the bottom of the Hue/Saturation box may shift slightly, indicating the exact range of colors you are about to affect. To extend the range of red, hold down the Shift key and sample from other parts of the phone box.

3. Move the Hue slider to the left or the right to change the color of the phone box. "Selections" don't come any easier!

So far, so good, but the cynics among you are probably thinking, Yeah, but what if there were other reds in the image that we didn't want affected? Once again layer masks are the answer. Take a look at this example:

A   B

FIGURE 5.15 The original image (example **A**) and the finished version with the color of the houseboat shifted (example **B**).

1. Open the Houseboat image. Here we want to shift the yellows of the house-boat, but obviously the yellows are not confined to the boat. No worries.

2. In the Hue/Saturation dialog box, choose Yellows from the Edit menu. Sample the color of the houseboat with the eyedropper, and then move the Hue slider to the left or the right until you find a color you like. Don't worry that the daffodils in the foreground are also affected—we'll fix that in the next step.

web files

A   B

FIGURE 5.16 Shifting the yellows also affects the daffodils in the foreground (examples **A** and **B**).

3. To restore the foreground to the way it was, choose a nice big, soft brush and paint on the layer mask of the Hue/Saturation adjustment layer in black.

FIGURE 5.17 Painting on the layer mask restores the foreground to its original colors.

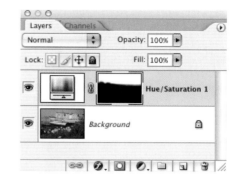

Will this approach work for any kind of image? Well, no. But it's worth a shot if your subject is a clearly identifiable primary color and is the only example of that color in the image, or at least can be easily isolated from other items of the same color.

Boosting Color

Another simple and effective use of Hue/Saturation is to boost a key color. Usually the effect should be subtle, but distinct enough to give the image an extra punch. If your image will be printed in CMYK, you might find it useful to turn on your Gamut Warning (View > Gamut Warning or Command/Ctrl-Shift-Y) to make sure that you don't introduce nonprintable colors into your image. Depending on whether the color you're affecting is spread throughout your image or isolated, you may or may not need to use a layer mask to restrict the adjustment layer to specific areas.

FIGURE 5.18 Boosting the yellow of the road markings (examples **A** and **B**) with a Hue shift (example **C**).

In the first two examples, the yellow was boosted easily without needing to use a layer mask.

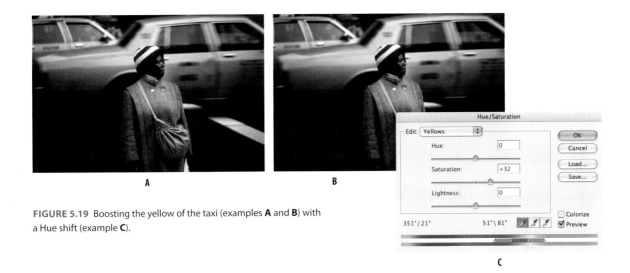

FIGURE 5.19 Boosting the yellow of the taxi (examples **A** and **B**) with a Hue shift (example **C**).

In the next example of a church and a sign, it's necessary to target the Hue shifts of the reds and the yellows with separate adjustment layers. While I could have made both changes on one adjustment layer, I separated the steps, making it clearer (to me at least) how the image was edited should I revisit it in the future. Because I wanted to reveal the color boost on less than 50% of the image, I then filled the layer mask with black, masking the effect of the adjustment layer. Then I switched my foreground color to white and painted on the layer mask with a soft-edged brush to reveal the boosted color in the signs.

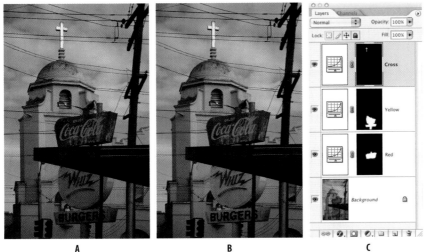

FIGURE 5.20 Boosting the red and yellow in the signs (examples **A** and **B**) and restricting the color shifts to specific areas using layer masks (example **C**).

Colorizing Images

For maximum control when colorizing grayscale images, use Hue/Saturation adjustment layers. Select the area to which you want to add color, and then choose Hue/Saturation from the adjustment layers pop-up menu at the bottom of the Layers palette. The selection becomes a layer mask on the adjustment layer, restricting the color to that area. In the Hue/Saturation dialog box, click the Colorize check box and experiment with the Hue slider (and possibly the Saturation and Lightness sliders).

FIGURE 5.21 Colorizing using Hue/Saturation adjustment layers and layer masks to specify where the color is applied.

A   B

Here are a few tips for using this technique:

- You must begin with an image in a color mode even if it looks black and white. If necessary choose Image > Mode > RGB or CMYK. If the image is already in a color mode, it helps to desaturate the image to remove any yellowing.

- Your currently chosen foreground color will determine your starting hue. So before creating the adjustment layer, choose a color that is within the range of what you're after. You must be on the image layer itself to choose colors.

- You can double-click the layer thumbnail to return to Hue/Saturation and adjust the color as necessary. Because the color is so easy to change, don't worry too much about finding the exact color right away. You may need to see the whole image in context of the colorizing to be able to determine the correct hue for each area.

- If you need to extend or restrict the effect of the color, you can paint on the layer mask in white or black, respectively.

- Where colors overlap, you can remove one from the other by Command/Ctrl-clicking the layer mask of the color you want to remove and (on the layer mask of the color you want to remove it from), filling or painting the selection with black. This means that you don't need to be accurate in painting an edge that meets another color, since you can subtract the selection of an existing mask from the paint you add.

- Occasionally viewing the layer mask by itself (Option/Alt-click on the layer mask) may be helpful to see exactly where the color is being applied.

Combining Color and Grayscale

Here's a technique that's fast, easy, economical, and effective: combine grayscale and color in the same image as a way of focusing attention on your subject. Feel free to use any of your own color images that needs focus in a particular area.

A   B

FIGURE 5.22 The original image (example **A**) and with the background desaturated (example **B**).

1. Make a selection of your subject.

2. Inverse the selection (Command/Ctrl-Shift-I or Select > Inverse).

3. Choose a Hue/Saturation adjustment layer and move the Saturation slider all the way to the left.

As an alternative to the first three steps, skip making the selection, desaturate the whole image with the adjustment layer, and then paint in black on the layer mask where you want to restore the color.

4. If you want the background to be in color and the subject in grayscale, target the layer mask of the Hue/Saturation adjustment layer and press Command/Ctrl-I to invert its values.

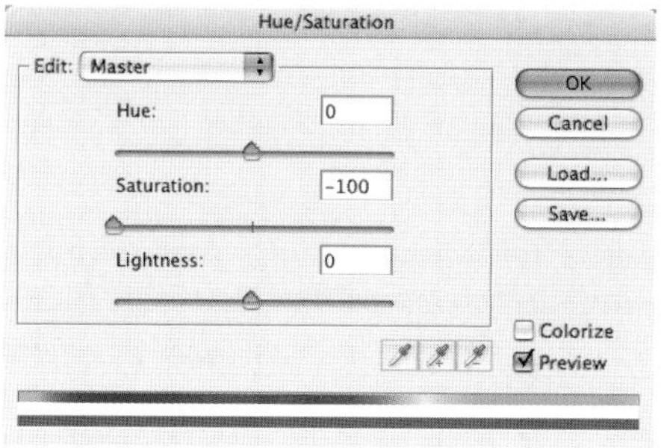

FIGURE 5.23 Use a Hue/Saturation adjustment layer to desaturate the color (example **A**), and then restore the areas of color by painting in black on the layer mask (example **B**).

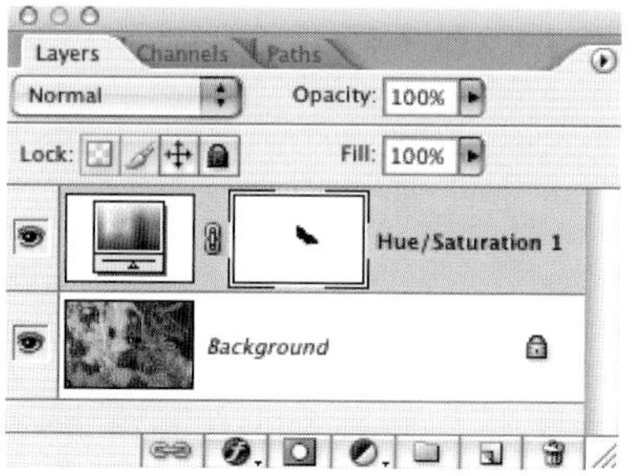

A

B

In Summary

There's more to selecting an image than defining an area with your selection tools. Before you get busy with your Magic Wand or Lassos, take a moment to evaluate the image and whether or not the selections you need are already there—implied by the color and tonal values of the image. Moreover, Curves and Hue/Saturation when applied as adjustment layers allow you to edit specific tones or colors without fear of damaging your original image. Throw in adjustment layer masks to restrict the effect of the adjustment layer and you have total control. And this is just the tip of the proverbial iceberg with adjustment layers. Try experimenting with Photo Filter to change the mood or to color correct your image. As we saw in the "Converting to Custom Grayscale" section of Chapter 2, Channel Mixer can be used to create custom grayscale images from color photos. Use Posterize in combination with layer mask to achieve Andy Warhol–like treatments of your image (great for handmade birthday cards). The key is that all your changes are reversible—turn off the adjustment layers and your original image is intact. With all this talk of nondestructive editing and the benefits of not being locked into a particular course of action you might think me a commitment-phobe. While you wouldn't be this first to call me this, a nondestructive workflow (of which adjustment layers form an essential part) is about far more than putting off or avoiding important decisions about your images. It's about maximizing your options, your creative freedom, and just making life easier.

CHAPTER 6

Channel Masking

SOME IMAGES DEFY EVEN THE MOST DEXTEROUS USE of the Pen tool, the most subtle choking of a layer mask, the most stealthy use of adjustment layers. You know the type of image I'm talking about: the woman with the frizzy hair, the flower arrangement with the seemingly infinite number of detailed edges, the dog or cat with the wispy fur. For such images we need a different approach: a channel mask.

The premise of channel masking is the same as that for "selecting" with adjustment layers: somewhere in your image is a built-in mask waiting to be teased out. For a channel mask the clues are in the color channels. The process involves copying whichever color channel has the most contrast between subject and background. This duplicate channel becomes an alpha channel—which you'll remember from Chapter 2 is a potential selection that can be loaded on an as-needed basis. Before loading the new alpha channel as a selection, use your Levels or Curves to heighten its contrast until subject and background are forced towards opaque white and black (or the other way around), with the white areas representing what is selected in the image and the black areas representing what is masked.

The reality isn't always so simple. Depending on how much contrast you begin with, teasing may be insufficient, and coercion may be necessary. Real world images rarely conform to average book examples. It's common for part of your subject to require the channel mask treatment, while other parts are better served by a more conventional selection approach. For example, the head of your curly haired subject may need a channel mask, but the body is sharply defined against the background. Mixing and matching is the name of the game.

Photoshop also has a special masking tool: Extract, found under the Filter menu or Command/Ctrl-Option/Alt-X, which you can use to cut out complex subjects from their backgrounds. And how come I haven't mentioned this until now? Well, because you can almost always get better results using conventional selection methods or channel masking.

Along with showing you my best practices for creating channel masks, this chapter will look at how, if you take a few extra steps, you can get good results with the Extract tool. For basic information about channels, see Chapter 2, "Channels."

Creating a Channel Mask: The Basics

Let's start with a simple channel masking example. Then we can get into the details of each step of this procedure.

1. Open the Westminster Abbey image. Before you do anything, ask yourself how you intend to use the image. How you plan to use the image once you've masked it will determine how accurate you need to make the mask.

web files

A   B

FIGURE 6.1 The original image (example **A**), and the image masked on a white background (example **B**).

2. Evaluate the channels to see which one offers the most contrast. Press Command/Ctrl-1, 2, 3, to look at the Red, Green, and Blue channels in turn. Select the channel that has the most edge contrast between subject and background—in this case Blue—and drag its thumbnail to the New icon at the bottom of the Channels palette to duplicate it. This duplicate channel is the basis for your mask.

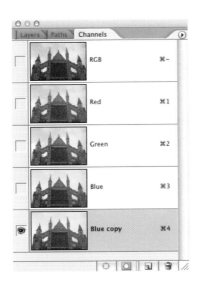

FIGURE 6.2 The Channels palette showing the duplicate Blue channel, the starting point of the mask.

3. Block out your mask: begin by viewing your duplicate channel and hiding all other channels. Choose your Brush tool and paint in any large areas in black or white, depending on whether these areas will become masked or selected areas. Alternatively, use the Lasso or Marquee tools to select and fill areas with black or white. Keep this step quick, creating a very basic separation between the black and white areas of your image. Stay away from any edges and use a hard-edged brush to avoid introducing any unwanted feathering into your mask.

FIGURE 6.3 Blocking out areas as opaque black and white on either side of the image edge.

4. Viewing your channel at 100%, force contrast by choosing Image > Adjustments > Levels and moving the Black point and White point sliders towards each other, into the center. Move the Midpoint slider to the right. Dark grays should become black, while the highlight areas become white. Watch how your adjustments are affecting the edges—if you overdo it by moving the Levels sliders too close together, the edges will lose detail and become aliased. Once you've applied your Level (or Curves) adjustment, you may need to paint in any small areas that didn't shift to black or white.

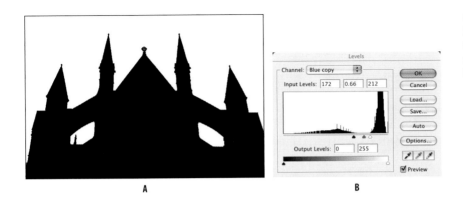

A   B

FIGURE 6.4 Applying a Levels adjustment to force the gray areas as far as possible towards opaque black and white.

5. Return to your RGB composite channel and load the mask as a selection by Command/Ctrl-clicking your duplicate channel (Alpha 1). You're now ready to use the selection any way you want. In this example we're going to turn it into a layer mask. Click the Add layer mask icon at the bottom of the Layers palette. Note that if you're working with a flattened image (i.e., one that has a background layer) you will first need to double-click the layer thumbnail to name the layer.

6. Refine the mask by painting on the layer mask to fix any inaccuracies. Of course, it's not until you put the image on top of another layer that the worst of the inaccuracies become obvious. In the examples that follow we see how to fix the edges of a mask when you are compositing the image with other layers.

FIGURE 6.5 Using a channel mask makes it easy to maintain fine detail around the edges of the building.

Creating a Channel Mask: The (Practical) Details

Create a channel mask in six easy steps is the theory. Of course, most images aren't as straightforward. Let's look at some tricks you can use when creating channel masks for more challenging images. Because every image presents a unique set of challenges, use these techniques as needed.

Determining Your Intent

Your intention for an image once you've masked it determines how accurate you need to make the mask. If you're preparing a cutout figure that will be placed in a page layout on white paper, your mask will be quite forgiving and may not need to be super-accurate. If, however, you're putting your cutout subject on a brightly colored background, perhaps with different lighting conditions, then every inaccuracy will be painfully obvious. If the masked subject will be composited with other layers, experiment with blend modes to conceal edge inaccuracies. Depending on the nature of your image and the layer or layers you are compositing it with, it may not be necessary to force the contrast to opaque black and white.

In the following example of a tree, the black parts of the mask are only 70% opaque in some places. This works because the original masked sky resembles the sky color of the background layer that replaces it. Not forcing the contrast makes it possible to retain as much of the fine detail in the branches and twigs as possible.

FIGURE 6.6 The original images (examples **A** and **B**), the finished composite (example **C**), and the mask (example **D**). Not forcing the contrast on the mask to opaque black and white retains more of the details in the tree branches. This works in this context because one blue sky is replacing another.

A

B

C

D

Choosing Your Channel

Choosing your channel is easiest when your image has a dominant color. The most obvious example is a blue sky, which can often be easily isolated using, not surprisingly, the Blue channel.

Color channels have different contrast in different color modes. If none of your RGB channels has enough contrast, try duplicating the image and converting it to CMYK to check the channels there. Once your image is in CMYK color mode, duplicate the channel with the most contrast. To use this duplicate channel, go to your original RGB image and choose Select > Load Selection, then choose the CMYK image as the source document, and select the appropriate channel from the Channel drop-down menu.

As an alternative to duplicating a channel, you may get better results using either of two options under the Image menu, Apply Image or Calculations, to make your alpha channel (a potential selection, stored in a channel as a grayscale image). Use Apply Image to combine a duplicate channel with any other channel or with itself, using the same blend mode options available for layers.

Calculations works slightly differently, letting you blend two individual channels (or two copies of the same channel) as a new channel. Both Apply Image and Calculate potentially yield the same result. For example, using Apply Image to apply the source Blue channel with a blend mode of Overlay to a duplicate (target) of the Blue channel is the same as using Calculations to blend the (source 1) Blue channel with itself (source 2) using Overlay blend mode.

For both options Overlay blend mode usually, but not always, works best, lightening values less than 50% gray and darkening values more than 50% gray.

FIGURE 6.7 The Apply Image (example **A**) and Calculations (example **B**) dialog boxes.

A

B

A   **B**

FIGURE 6.8 A copy of the Blue channel (example **A**), and a more contrasty result using Calculations to blend the Blue channel with itself using the Overlay blend mode (example **B**).

FIGURE 6.9 The original image (example **A**), and a duplicate of its Blue channel (example **B**). Adding a temporary Curves adjustment layer to increase the contrast (example **C**) and duplicating the Blue channel using Calculations yield a much more contrasty alpha channel (example **D**)—a better starting point for your channel mask.

You can make it easier to choose your channel mask by adding more contrast to your image with a temporary adjustment layer. Add a Curves adjustment layer and pull the curve down in the shadows and up in the highlights to increase the contrast. Now, when you view your color channels one of them should have the contrast you need. Once you have made (or calculated) your duplicate channel and refined it into a mask, you can trash the adjustment layer. Note that you can also use this approach to help out any of your Selection tools.

A   **B**

C   **D**

Blocking Out

In step 3 of "Creating a Channel Mask," I advised that when painting on your mask you should stay well away from the edges. In some circumstances, however, you can paint up to the edges. If an edge already has a good amount of contrast, try painting in Overlay blend mode. Painting in white in Overlay blend mode turns the gray areas white, but leaves the black areas unaffected; painting in black has the opposite effect. We saw this in "Using Quick Mask to Paint Selections" in Chapter 2, "Channels."

Forcing Contrast

Make sure that what looks like black is actually black (100%) and what looks like white is actually white (0%) by opening your Info palette and taking a tour around the edges with your Eyedropper tool to note the exact gray values. You may find it helpful to Shift-click a couple of places to take color samples of your edge areas. These samples remain fixed so that you can compare the before and after values on the Info palette.

Note that if you don't want sharp edges, then forcing your mask to opaque black and white is neither necessary nor desirable.

Because the gray values of your edges may vary, some parts of the edge may require more force than others to turn them black or white. Here are the steps you can take to force contrast.

1. Try making a selection of as much of the edge as is similar in gray values and applying a Curve; then repeat, adjusting the Curve only as much as necessary for each selection.

   Those of you with strong constitutions can attempt to use Curves in Arbitrary mode to draw the shape of the curve.

2. To draw the curve, begin by locking points onto the Curve at the darkest and lightest points of the channel by Command/Ctrl-clicking with the eyedropper. Now take the Pencil tool and draw the bottom left of the curve in to the right until it is vertically aligned beneath your first sample point (highlight). Repeat for the top right of the curve until it is vertically aligned beneath your shadow sample point. You may find it helpful to click the Smooth button a couple of times to smooth out any kinks in the curve.

FIGURE 6.10 Using the Curve pencil to draw an arbitrary curve. The anchor points on the curve indicate the sampled areas of the image— one for the light grays and one for the dark grays.

3. Rather than force the contrast on an alpha channel, make your duplicate channel into a layer mask and work on it there. If you are combining the masked image with the layers below it, this is a more interactive way of evaluating how the image will look in the context of the overall composition. I find it useful to do my "first draft" mask as an alpha channel (and as a "base mask," I can refer back to it), and then convert it to a layer mask to further refine it, in the context of the other layers in the composition.

Alternatively, turn on the visibility of your composite RGB channel so that the alpha channel appears as a color overlay. You can paint in the mask as if it were a Quick Mask.

FIGURE 6.11 Turn on the visibility of your RGB composite channel to view the channel mask (as a color overlay) in the context of the image.

4. Use the Median filter, one of Photoshop's noise reduction filters (Filter > Noise > Median) at its lowest value—1 pixel—to pick up any stray pixels on your channel mask.

FIGURE 6.12 Using the Median filter to remove any stray pixels, before (example **A**) and after (example **B**).

A · B

Refining the Mask

Now's the time to let slip the dogs of war on your mask in progress. Or at least to bring out all your masking tricks. Consider these strategies for particularly tricky situations.

All-Purpose Strategies to Edit Your Mask

Be realistic. It's easy to lose hours trying to make the perfect mask. To paraphrase Gen. George Patton, "A good mask today is better than a perfect mask tomorrow." And remember the old adage of experienced Photoshop maskers everywhere: "No one sees what you leave out." Sometimes you can't include every strand of hair, so don't drive yourself crazy trying. Ironically, including every last detail may actually make the result look fake. We're after the greater truth here, and if that involves leaving out a strand or two of hair, then so be it. Your subject probably needed a haircut anyway.

Channel masking (when it works) is such an elegant and pleasing technique that you will want to use it all the time. But don't throw away your Selection tools. Stay flexible and open to all possibilities. For example, a channel mask may be just the ticket for the head, but when it comes to the shoulders and torso, you may be better off using your conventional Selection tools.

To get the best results when editing your mask, combine the following techniques and strategies as needed.

Put Your Subject on a Temporary Color Layer

Highlight any problems with your mask by creating a new layer and dragging it beneath your image layer. Fill this layer with a bright color like neon orange or lime green. Warning: This will probably look ghastly. When you have made any necessary adjustments, you can delete the color layer.

FIGURE 6.13 Use a temporary color layer to bring out problems in the mask.

Choking the Mask

We've detailed this technique in "Choking the Mask" in Chapter 4, "Layer Masks." You can try to apply it here, although presumably most of its potential will have been exhausted in the earlier section in this chapter, "Forcing Contrast."

Using the Blur and Sharpen Tools to Fix Edges

To selectively blur or (less likely) selectively sharpen parts of your mask edge, use the Blur (r) or Sharpen (r) tools on your layer mask. Choose a soft-edged brush and paint around the edges, adjusting the brush Strength as necessary. Alternatively, you can try making a selection on your mask of the edges you want blurred and apply a Gaussian Blur filter. To vary the softness, make several small selections, rather than one big one, and apply varying amounts of blurring. Both this and the previous technique of choking the mask are best done with the final background in place because the image context will determine the amount required.

Defringing with Blend Modes

Depending on the lighting conditions of your image you may be able to use blend modes to fix color fringing around fine details. The most likely blend modes to work will be Multiply or Hard Light. Indeed, if your image is a silhouette you may be able to get away with just using these without a channel mask. With the image of the London Eye on the next page, we see all kinds of nasty fringing around the fine details when we place the masked image on an alternative sky.

FIGURE 6.14 The original image (example **A**). The masked image on a white background looks OK (example **B**), but when viewed against another image layer the fringing is evident (examples **C** and **D**).

A

B

C

D

1. Open the London Eye image.

2. Make a channel mask based on a duplicate of the Blue channel using the steps outlined earlier in "Creating a Channel Mask: The Basics." I have included a pre-made alpha channel with this image if you want to skip this step.

web files

3. Load the alpha channel—yours or the one that is saved with the image—and convert the resulting selection into a layer mask revealing the sky layer beneath.

4. To fix the fringing, duplicate the image layer, delete the layer mask from the duplicate layer, and turn its blend mode to Hard Light. This fixes the fringing but makes the image too dark.

FIGURE 6.15 Adding a Hard Light layer fixes one problem but creates another—the image is now too dark.

5. To address the too-dark image, add a Curves adjustment layer above the original image layer to brighten the detail. To avoid also brightening the sky, I clipped this adjustment layer to the transparency of the layer beneath—hold down Option/Alt and click the horizontal line separating the layers.

FIGURE 6.16 The finished image (example **A**), and its Layers palette showing how it is composed (example **B**).

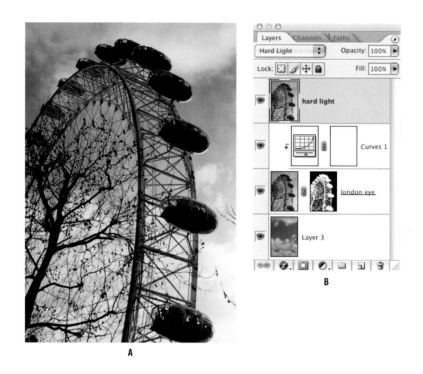

A

B

Here's another example using that holy grail of masking: a curly haired subject. Such images typically require a good deal of experimentation and may take you down some blind alleys. Here's what worked for me in this particular case.

I began with these two images. If you like, you can follow along with your own suitable images.

FIGURE 6.17 The image layers: a curly-haired subject and the Golden Gate Bridge.

ISTOCKPHOTO.COM

1. Start with your frizzy-haired subject, using a channel mask to isolate the hair. In my example, the initial channel mask, though a good start, shows color fringing problems when the image is seen in the context of its new background.

FIGURE 6.18 The channel mask (example **A**) used to mask the subject (example **B**). A close-up showing the color fringing problems (example **C**), and the Layers palette showing how the image is constructed (example **D**).

A

B

C

D

2. To fix the color fringing, duplicate the image layer and its layer mask and set the blend mode of the duplicate layer to Multiply. This goes some way towards fixing the problem, but makes the image too dark.

3. To correct the dark image, switch the stacking order of the layers, placing the original image layer above the Multiply layer. Then, on the layer mask of the original layer, paint in black around the edges of the hair, hiding the hair on that layer and revealing the hair from the Multiply layer below. This is an improvement, but now the hair has a translucent quality that looks fake.

FIGURE 6.19 Painting on the layer mask of the image layer reveals the fine strands of hair on the Multiply layer beneath, but now the hair looks oddly transparent.

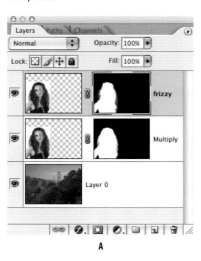

A

B

4. To fix the transparency, duplicate the Multiply layer and move the copy above the image layer. The original image layer is now sandwiched top and bottom by a duplicated Multiply layer. On this top layer, I painted out most of the detail of the figure on the layer mask, leaving just the fine edges of the hair, and building density and opacity with the other Multiply layer below.

A

B

C

FIGURE 6.20 A Multiply sandwich: a second Multiply layer on top of the layer stack (example **A**) reveals just the fine edges of the hair (examples **B** and **C**).

Another approach to correct color fringing uses the Color blend mode and paints around the edges of your masked subject on a separate layer. This tends to work best when the subject is fairly uniform in color. The image of a palm tree on page 234 is a good example.

1. Open the Palm Tree image.

web files

FIGURE 6.21 The original photo of the palm tree (example **A**) and the masked version (example **B**).

A   B

2. Create a channel mask using the steps outlined in the previous section, "Creating a Channel Mask."

3. Turn the channel mask into a layer mask by first loading it as a selection (drag its thumbnail onto the Load channel as selection icon at the bottom of the Channels palette) and then click the Add Layer Mask at the bottom of the Layers palette.

4. Create a temporary color layer to highlight the color fringing problems.

5. Add a new layer above the image layer and make its blend mode Color. Call this layer Fix Fringing. This layer needs to be clipped by the layer below, so hold down Option/Alt and click the line between the layers to make a clipping mask.

6. With your Eyedropper tool sample the color from just inside the edges of the palm tree where there is no fringing.

7. Choose a brush size appropriate for the size of your edge and paint over the edge. The blue fringe is painted green to match the tree. Because the defringing layer is clipped by the layer below, the paint will be masked by the image layer's transparency. To put it another way, paint will only go where there's already paint.

8. Experiment with the opacity of the Fix Fringing layer. The Color blend mode works well in this example, but won't with every type of image.

9. If the Color blend mode doesn't give the desired results, experiment with Multiply or Darken. Which mode will work will depend on what colors you're working with.

A   B

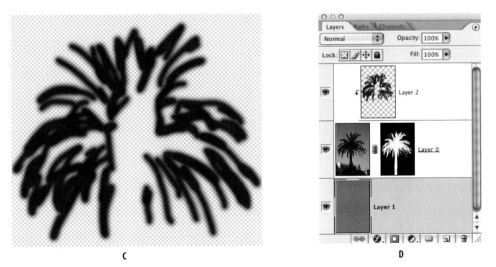

C   D

FIGURE 6.22 The masked palm tree on a color background shows blue color fringing (example **A**). Painting on a clipped layer above with color sampled from the palm tree fixes the problem (examples **B**, **C**, and **D**).

A variation of this technique is to use the Clone Stamp tool instead of the Brush, making sure that the Sample All Layers option and Aligned options are checked. Clone from just inside the subject edge (where there is no color fringing) onto the edge itself.

Masking Glass

Masking transparent objects requires a slightly different approach. Forcing the contrast on the duplicate channel to opaque white will cause the glass to become opaque. Assuming that you want to mask the background completely, force the contrast of the shadow areas to black, but leave the highlight areas light gray. That way, when you convert the channel to a layer mask you'll be able to see through your subject to the layer below. Take a look at this example.

web files

1. Open the Martini Glass and Wall images.

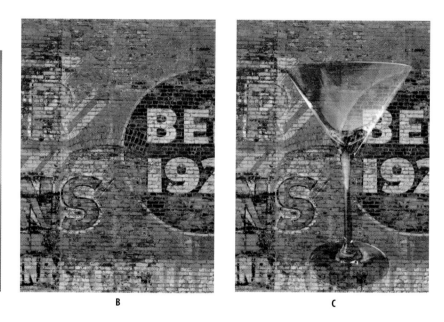

A   B   C

FIGURE 6.23 Start with a martini glass and a wall background (examples **A** and **B**) to create a finished composite (example **C**).

2. Drag the martini glass onto the background image. Turn off the visibility of the Background layer.

3. Choose Image > Calculations and combine the Red channel (the one with the most contrast) with itself using the Overlay blend mode to create a new channel, Alpha 1. In this case, you're using Calculations to blend two copies of the same channel.

4. Still on your duplicate (the new Alpha) channel, draw a pen path around the glass. Choose Make Selection from the Paths palette menu to turn the path into a selection. I used a 1-pixel feather radius.

5. Inverse the selection (Select > Inverse or Command/Ctrl-I) and fill the alpha channel with black to block out the background. Deselect your selection.

FIGURE 6.24 The channel mask with the background filled with black.

6. Still on the Alpha 1 channel, lighten the midtone grays of the channel to make the glass more "see-through" when composited with another layer. I used Curves and pulled the Curve down from the midpoint, but using Levels and moving the Midpoint slider to the left would also work.

7. Return to your composite RGB channel and load Alpha 1 as a selection by dragging its thumbnail onto the Load channel as selection icon at the bottom of the Channels palette.

8. Click the Add Layer Mask icon at the bottom of the Layers palette to convert the selection to a layer mask.

9. To soften the mask edge, choke the layer mask by applying a 1.5 pixel Gaussian Blur and then, using Levels, move the Black and Gray point slider to the right.

FIGURE 6.25 The glass masked but lacking definition.

Now we're ready to return some definition to the glass, which was lost in the flat gray values in the layer mask.

10. Make sure that the visibility of the Background layer is turned off. Choose Select > Color Range and choose Midtones from the Sampled Colors drop down menu. Click OK to return to your image.

FIGURE 6.26 Selecting the midtones using Color Range.

11. Copy this active selection to a new layer (Command/Ctrl-J) and name this layer Midtones.

12. So that the Midtones layer is clipped by the Glass layer, hold down Option/Alt and click the horizontal line separating the layers.

13. Change the Blend mode of the Midtones layer to Linear Burn and experiment with the Opacity of the layer. Why Linear Burn? Well, it just worked best in this situation.

14. To prevent blending mode changes to the Midtones layer from affecting the Background layer, select both the Glass and the Midtones layer, and from the Layers palette menu choose New Group from Layers.

15. Add a Curve adjustment layer as necessary to brighten the glass.

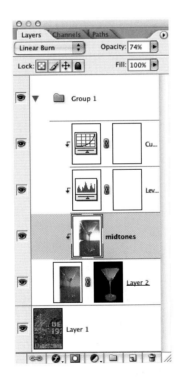

FIGURE 6.27 The Layers palette of the image showing how the image is constructed.

Extracting Subjects

Some people love the Extract tool. I'm not one of them. If you master all the other selection techniques we've discussed, you'll almost always get a better (and quicker) result than by using Extract. That said, Extract is a viable alternative to channel masks when cutting out complex subjects..

Before we look at the finer points, let's step through the Extract process. Try this on any of your own images with a hairy subject against a low contrast background.

1. Always begin by duplicating your layer (Command/Ctrl-J) to protect your image. Extract deletes unwanted portions of an image rather than masking them.

2. To access the Extract tool, choose Filter > Extract (Command/Ctrl-Option/Alt-X). Highlight the edges of the subject to be extracted by drawing around it with the Highlighter tool. The default highlight color is green. Change the width of the highlighter according to the type of edge transition. Extract looks for the difference in contrast between pixels in the foreground and background of your selection, so make sure that the highlight overlaps both the foreground and background areas along the edge. Be sure to include any interior areas of transition. The fatter the brush, the more touch-up you'll have to do, although fatter brushes make for easy (and sloppy) selections. If your subject goes to the edges of your canvas, you don't need to outline along the edge. Smart Highlighting varies the width of the highlighter and works best if the edge is well defined. If you go wrong, hold down Option/Alt to toggle to the Eraser tool.

FIGURE 6.28 The original image (example **A**), and outlined with the Extract tool Highlighter (example **B**).

A

B

3. Once the outline is drawn, switch to the Paint Bucket and click inside the object to fill within your selection. The default Fill color is blue.

FIGURE 6.29 The subject filled with the Paint Bucket.

4. Preview. At the bottom right of the Extract window you can select various options to preview the extracted subject against different backgrounds, show the object's highlight or fill, or switch between the original and extracted image.

FIGURE 6.30 The Extracted subject.

5. Refine and touch up the image using the Cleanup tool and the Edge Touchup tools, which only become available after you click the Preview button. The Cleanup tool subtracts opacity, with multiple passes having a cumulative effect. To restore opacity, hold down Option/Alt. The Edge Touchup tool sharpens the edges of the extracted image by adding opacity to the image or making the background more transparent.

6. Once you're satisfied with the result, click OK to apply the extraction.

For best results with Extract, you'll want to take a few extra steps, either with a layer mask or alpha channel.

Refining Extracted Edges with a Layer Mask

It's worth using the Extract Touchup tools to fix any obvious problems with your extraction, but for fine-tuning you'll also want to use a layer mask. Here's how.

1. Follow steps 1 through 6 of the previous section, "Extracting Subjects," to duplicate your original layer and make the extraction on the duplicate layer.

2. Load the transparency mask from the extracted layer by Command/Ctrl-clicking the layer thumbnail and turn this selection into a layer mask on the unextracted layer. (If this is a Background layer, Option/Alt double-click its thumbnail to convert it to a normal layer.)

3. Now that it has served its purpose, delete the extracted layer.

4. With the layer mask, use your full repertoire of masking tricks to refine the edges—restoring any lost parts by painting in white, selectively blurring parts of the edge by painting on the layer mask with the Blur tool, and spreading or choking the mask using Levels or Curves.

FIGURE 6.31 A bright color layer underneath the image layer highlighting any edge problems (example **A**) and the extracted layer as the basis for the layer mask (example **B**).

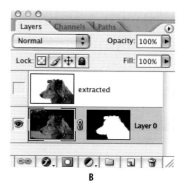

A

B

Using Extract with an Alpha Channel

Here's a handy technique for combining the precision of the Pen tool with the capabilities of Extract, devised by Russell Brown, the wacky professor of Photoshop. It combines the Extract techniques we have used thus far with an alternative, more accurate, method of highlighting the edge of your subject. Because using the Extract Highlighter tool can be a bit hit or miss, you can get more predictable results if you use an alpha channel derived from a pen path as the basis for your extraction.

FIGURE 6.32 The original tiger image (example **A**) and the extracted version (example **B**).

1. Before we can extract our subject, we need to prepare our image. Draw a pen path around your subject. Double-click the Work Path thumbnail in the Paths palette to save the path.

2. Duplicate your layer (Command/Ctrl-J). It's this duplicate (unextracted) layer to which we will later add a layer mask.

3. Create a new channel (Alpha 1) by clicking the New Channel icon at the bottom of the Channels palette. The new channel will be black. Make your foreground color white, choose your Brush tool and a 20-pixel brush at 50% hardness. With your saved path active, click the Stroke Path with Brush icon at the bottom of the Paths palette.

4. Invert the channel (Command/Ctrl-I). Your channel should now be white with the shape of your subject outlined in black. It is this outline that we will use instead of the Extract Highlighter tools to define the subject.

5. Now that the image is prepped, choose Filter > Extract (Command/Ctrl-Option/Alt-X). In the Extract dialog box, choose Alpha 1 from the Channel drop-down menu as your outline and proceed with Extraction as above in "Extracting Subjects," steps 3 through 6.

FIGURE 6.33 Stroking a path on a new channel (example **A**), inverting the channel (example **B**), and then using it as an alternative to the Highlighter tool (example **C**).

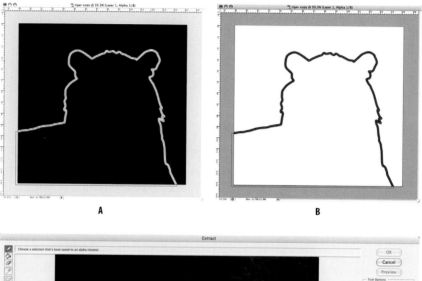

A

B

C

FIGURE 6.34 The resulting extraction.

6. Once you're satisfied with the extraction, fine-tune the edges using a layer mask as outlined in steps 2 through 4 of the previous technique, "Refining Extracted Edges with a Layer Mask."

In Summary

Channel masks are the jewel in the crown of your selection tools. Sometimes they can make easy work of an impossible-looking selection. And when they work you feel like you've arrived—in Photoshop terms at least. Because every image is unique, there are no off-the-shelf, one-size-fits-all solutions. But after experimenting with channel masks you'll quickly develop an instinct for when they are the best way to tackle the job and for what other techniques, if any, you may need to use. Basically, if the subject of your image has fine edges, a dominant color, and reasonably good edge contrast, then a channel mask will work. If not, then perhaps a channel mask is still appropriate for part of the selection.

Index